WHAT PEOPLE LEADERS A
THE BIG QUIT SURVIVAL GuiDE

"The timing of this book couldn't be better. Merrylue Martin doesn't just tell leaders what is needed to engage and keep their top performers, she provides an amazing set of tools on HOW to do it."

Daniel Galster, Sr. Manager, Charles Schwab

"It's simple, yet complex. In order for employees to want to stay in a job, they need to feel their employer respects their physical, emotional, financial, and social health. In *The BIG QUIT Survival Guide*, Merrylue Martin demonstrates the importance of this and how employers can effectively make it happen."

Ed Bray, Sr. Director, HR, Ross Stores, Inc., and award-winning author of *Hello, Job Search* and *Hello, Career*

"Merrylue Martin's humor, down-to-earth style, and master storytelling will capture the reader, and are but a few of the attributes that make her a sought-after leadership guru. Her first-hand practical knowledge will help any leader attract, motivate, and retain top performers, and best of all, her lessons can be put into action DAY ONE!"

Kimberly Jackson, Chief of Staff, City Attorney's Office City of San Jose, California

"Merrylue creates a template of creativity and strategy that results in business success and happy employees."

Jennifer Zanetich, AVP Talent & Organizational Effectiveness Virtua Health

"Dr. Martin has had a profound impact on thousands of people leaders nationwide during her career. She has a unique perspective on what causes turnover and, more importantly, what to do about it. Her book is a gift to any leader looking to survive the Great Resignation!"

John Boyens, Co-Founder/President, Boyens Group Inc.

TOOLS AND TACTICS
TO ATTRACT THE BEST,
RETAIN TOP PERFORMERS &
NAIL THE TALENT WAR

THE BIG QUIT SURVIVAL GUIDE

MERRYLUE MARTIN

ISBN (paperback) 979-8-9855976-0-8
ISBN (hardcover) 979-8-9855976-3-9
ISBN (ebook) 979-8-9855976-1-5
ISBN (audiobook) 979-8-9855976-2-2

Library of Congress Control Number: 2022902245

Cover design: Alexander Ness, Nessgraphica
Interior design: Megan McCullough
Graphics: Hanna Tamsalu-Orlova
Editorial services: Sandra Wendel, Write On, Inc.

Published by the Job Joy Group, LLC
Carmel, Indiana
www.BigQuitSurvivalGuide.com

To all people leaders who regrettably lost a top performer—

and may still be wondering why.

CONTENTS

PART I   WHAT GOT US HERE?

PART II GOING MENTAL: THE PSYCHOLOGY OF WORK

PART III   WILL I STAY OR WILL I GO? (YES, BUT IT DEPENDS)

PART IV BALANCED FROM THE BEGINNING

WHO SHOULD READ THIS BOOK?

This book is about the intricate balancing act of keeping top performers. It's for people leaders who need to meet their most valued employees' expectations and at the same time deliver business results. It's about understanding how top performers will decide to stay or leave your company or organization by balancing what the job requires them to do with what they are getting in return, and the respect they are feeling while doing it—all the while occurring in a workplace setting that has been flipped upside down from a pandemic and other market factors.

MAIN PARTS OF THE BOOK

Part I What Got Us Here?

Provides a historical context of the decades of workplace cultures that have led up to the events of the last two years with a record number of people leaving their jobs during a pandemic. Explores various ways organizations have attempted to determine employee engagement and specific reasons driving turnover and the varying degree of success with each approach when used in the past.

Part II   Going Mental: The Psychology of Work

Takes a look at what is driving current employees' behavior through a psychological lens of basic human needs and motivation theory. Works from the basic foundation that people are *people*, first, and employees second. This area also covers the issue of stress and burnout and provides people leaders with ways to assess warning signs and provide timely interventions.

Part III Will I Stay or Will I Go? (Yes, but It Depends)

Reveals how employees choose to stay by determining whether the Requirements being asked of them balance with the Rewards and Respect they are getting in return—a construct introduced in this book and referred to as the 3-R scale. Four possible outcomes of the 3-R scale are discussed with the varying degrees of flight risk associated with each. If you want to go directly to the retention success formulas, start here.

Part IV Balanced from the Beginning

Many factors will impact the balance of an employee's 3-R scale. Recruiting and onboarding experiences, culture, relationship with their leader, and working remotely can all have a positive or negative effect. Each of these factors will be reviewed with guidelines on how to set up an employee's 3-R scale early on for optimal balance going forward.

TAKE FIVE

The TAKE FIVE section at the end of each chapter provides a quick summary for those who would like to skim the book and pick up the five main points in each chapter.

Survival Tactics

At the end of each chapter following the TAKE FIVE section are a number of Survival Tactics to help you quicky put into action what you will learn. Activities include self-assessments, question guides, checklists, team building ideas, and best practices. Exclusively for readers of this book: Download a user-friendly copy of the BIG QUIT Survival Kit that contains all the Survival Tactics in a printable 8½ x 11–size format. Go to www.BigQuitSurvivalGuide.com, click on the *Download Survival Kit* tab and enter the password: survival.

ROLE DEFINITIONS USED IN THIS BOOK

There can be several definitions of the terms used in this book. For use in this context, they are defined as follows:

People leaders

Those who lead teams of people in organizations of all types and sizes and who depend on the success of those teams to meet business goals.

Leader

The term *leader* here includes both strategic thinking skills and tactical managerial tasks. People leaders continuously do both.

High potentials

Employees in the top talent pool who have demonstrated early traits of leadership and are noted in succession plans to become future leaders. They are the most eager to grow and learn.

Top performers

Employees in the top talent pool who have a proven record of leadership capabilities as well as achieving business results. They continue to provide value above what is expected. Keeping them is critical and therefore the primary focus of this book.

Top talent

Refers to an elite pool of employees who have been identified as high potentials or top performers.

WELCOME TO THE NEW WORKPLACE

What a difference a global pandemic makes. Workplaces used to buzz with life in physical locations. Meeting facilities and conference rooms were booked weeks or even months out. Business travel was part of the everyday norm. Organizations focused on meeting business goals, and people leaders focused on coaching their employees to achieve their next personal best.

And then in an instant it all changed.

There went the playbooks with all the workplace norms as we knew them, and many top performers disappeared right along with them as well. While it remains to be seen what parts of the old normal will return, if anything, all we can bet on for the foreseeable future is that everything is completely different now.

No one in the labor market has been immune from the fallout of the Great Resignation or Turnover Tsunami as it's been called. If you're a people leader in a large corporation, small business, government sector, or nonprofit, you are likely still feeling the aftershocks while you assess the damage, sift through the shards, and begin gluing the workplace pieces back together only to discover the old pieces aren't quite fitting the same way as they used to.

Yes, more people have recently left their jobs in record numbers and, yes, in the lower paying sectors may continue to do so, and we continue to read they are never coming back. To an extent that is true. Those pushing retirement prior to the pandemic decided to do so early. Some of your former employees are retraining for new careers. Many have started their own businesses as record numbers of applications for LLCs and sole proprietorships have been filed. Some are looking to enter higher paying industries, and others have simply dropped out of work in search of more meaningful purpose and fulfillment, at least until the money runs out.

But in the middle of this Great Resignation, we're also starting to see something else brewing. It's looking more like a Great Reemergence or maybe a Great Reset or a Greater Reshuffling. Dare we say there may be some actual hope among all the dismal labor shortage statistics? There's even some chatter about the coming Great Rebound where the top talent who once fled to greener pastures have since decided there's no place like home and want to come back.

People will return to work, just not with the same mindset they had when they left. For many employees the pandemic struck a nerve about the fragility of life and prompted a renewed sense of purpose and clarity. Work is now only one of the many puzzle pieces that must appropriately fit into the overall picture they define as "life."

The companies that understand this renewing of the mind that's occurring and are willing to put the processes in place to support it will be the winners in attracting and keeping the top talent that's waiting to land. So get ready to welcome them and jump on rebuilding a workplace that will continue to attract and keep your best people going forward.

If your talent has stayed with you through these past several months, now is certainly the time to make sure you're doing everything in your power to keep them. If you've lost top performers, rest assured there's plenty of talent still out there looking, but they are taking their time and being intentional about their next employment move.

The purpose of this book is to help people leaders navigate the new work environment, fully grasp what is going on inside the reemerging employee's mindset, and understand what it will take to attract and keep them. In many ways the pandemic has also become the Great Catalyst.

As the dust continues to settle, we will see many positive changes and outcomes resulting in stronger, more authentic, and productive work environments. Employees are returning with different expectations. How we successfully engage with them will be different, and keeping them will certainly take a different approach. To get a quick sense of what this "different" might look like for people leaders, consider these true or false questions. If you want to find out now how you did, jump to chapter 17 to see the answers.

T	F	I am confident that each of my top performers feels they are getting the right balance of respect and rewards in return for the work required of them.
T	F	The team leader is primarily responsible for their employees' retention.
T	F	What employees want most right now is empathy.
T	F	Respect is defined differently by the person receiving it; therefore, I am aware of what it uniquely means to each of my employees.
T	F	Remote employees need just as much attention as those on-site.

On the surface some of these statements may appear obvious or maybe not. If you had to think about a couple of them, that's the idea. For example, if you answered false to the last question, excellent choice! Remote employees need more attention from you than your on-site people in order to counterbalance some of the unique challenges they are facing, like isolation. These questions and many others about how to navigate this new workplace and employees' expectations are addressed throughout the book.

One of the most important concepts to grasp up front is the emphasis employees are placing on the need for organizations to care for them as human beings. We are hearing a lot on this topic lately and will continue to do so as mental wellness and taking a holistic view of employees as people is now becoming one of the basic tenets in today's workplace. Simply put, the old physical has become the new psychological. Employees no longer place as much value on physical perks as they did in the past. Free food, Ping-Pong tables, and gym memberships have been traded for nonnegotiables such as respect, appreciation, and mental care.

Another key word emerging strongly in this new workplace is *balance*. Employees are on a mission for work-life balance. They are regularly assessing this balance and will weigh in on their desire to stay with a job by asking themselves three key questions:

1. What is it costing me physically and psychologically to succeed at this job? (Requirements)

2. What am I tangibly getting in return for doing this job? (Rewards)

3. How appreciated, trusted, and valued do I feel on this job? (Respect)

Picture a teeter-totter–type scale. On one side of the scale sits the Requirements weight. On the other side sit the Rewards and Respect weights. If the combined weight of the Rewards and Respect at least meets the weight of the Requirements, the scale will balance. If the Requirements weight is heavier than the combined Rewards and Respect weights, the scale will not balance and end up tilting under the weight of the Requirements. Employees with a balanced scale will likely stay. Those whose scale is collapsing under the Requirements weight will likely leave. Simple as that. Yes, but not so fast.

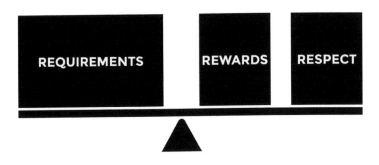

The 3-R balanced scale.

The three weights can be calibrated to create balance, but because each employee is unique, the heaviness factor they assign to the individual components within each of the weights will vary. For example, the Requirements may include a necessity to make a one-hour commute. The thought of this might be torturous for one employee but for another may be a welcomed chance to decompress and listen to a complete podcast without interruption. Therefore, it's crucial that people leaders have ongoing conversations with their employees—especially with the top talent they want to protect and keep—to determine what will impact the balance of their scale and ways it can be calibrated as needed to get it back in balance as soon as possible.

Turnover is not always a negative outcome to be avoided at all costs. Those employees who were not suitable hires or deteriorated into nonperformers with no desire to improve need to be gone. But when it comes to keeping your best people, that's a different story, and you want to do everything in your power to do so. The bad news about employee retention is that it's tricky because it deals with employees who also happen to be people, and people can be complex.

The comforting news about employee retention is that because it deals with people, we know for a fact that all people have basic needs in common and that's an effective place to start. While specific solutions for meeting those needs may differ for each individual, the fact remains that the types of needs humans have will always remain constant.

I don't know about you, but any constant in this workplace right now is a welcomed data point when it comes to cracking the employee retention code.

Consider this situation:

OPENING SCENE

"Last Week's 1:1 Meeting"

Setting: Late afternoon. Jessie, a sales manager with a medical supply company, leads a team of 11 sales reps. Tam is Jessie's star performer, four years running. Their weekly 1:1 meeting is about to begin.

Jessie: (waves Tam in to sit at the conference table while finishing up a phone conversation) *I'm hoping for a positive outcome though, with Judson in our camp. Will do. Okay. Gotta run. Thanks, you too. Bye."* (hangs up, sits down with Tam) *Hey, Tam, sorry about that. Been out in the field all day and just now returning the morning calls. Can I get you a water?*

Tam: *No problem—thanks, I'm good.*

Jessie: *So, how's it going?*

Tam: *Good, crazy busy as always. I was finally able to see the head of purchasing at North. Had a good conversation. Looks like we'll close the PO by the end of the week.*

Jessie: *Outstanding! You've done an amazing job there, in just a few weeks. Nice work, Tam.*

Tam: *Thanks. Yeah, it's been tricky with all the personnel changes going on there.*

Jessie: *Seriously, that's awesome. Do you want to run through the rest of the Q4 pipeline?*

Tam: *Ah, sure, we can, but I first wanted to take our conversation in a different direction.*

Jessie: *Um, okay, what's on your mind?*

Tam: *You know, I can't believe I'm coming up on 5 years and—*

Jessie: (interrupts Tam) *I know, absolutely. Not to mention you've doubled your territory revenue year over year for the past four of them. Without a doubt, Tam, you continue to be one of the most important players on this team.*

Tam: *And I appreciate that, Jessie, but to be honest, I haven't exactly been feeling that way very much lately.*

Jessie: *What do you mean?*

Tam: *Well, you know these past 6 months have been crazy for everyone, and we're all running in a million directions. But personally, it feels the more effort I keep putting out to carry all the extra projects has now sort of just settled into the norm of what's expected and with no additional considerations. I guess what I'm saying is, the load is twice as heavy, the return is twice as light, and keeping up at the pace expected is—*

Jessie: (interrupts Tam) *I know, Tam. I completely get it. It's been nuts lately and you've been great about it. Hey, once we get fully staffed, the pace will get back to normal, I promise, but I didn't realize you were feeling this way, though, so I'm glad we're having this conversation.*

Tam: *Well, you know me, I'm one that doesn't like to complain. I'll just do what it takes to make sure it all works. But I have to say,*

I think the real rub started 3 months ago when my mom was so sick and needed my help. Instead of getting approval to work remotely, I had to use up all my PTO instead. That really burned, Jessie, and you know first-hand, I wasn't happy about it.

Jessie: *Yeah, I know, and I am sorry it ended up that way. Believe me I tried my best for a different outcome, but unfortunately, it was company policy, and my hands were tied.*

Tam: *I get that, Jessie, and I'm not blaming you totally. It's more of a combination of things.*

Jessie: *Okay. I hear you, so how do we fix it? What can I do to make it right going forward?*

Tam: *I appreciate that, Jessie, but that's what I'm coming to. There isn't anything at this point. It's too late for that. I just accepted another opportunity and am submitting my 2 weeks' notice.* (hands Jessie the resignation letter)

Jessie: *What?*

Tam: *This is hard because I did thrive here and loved my accounts. I've been wrestling with this decision for a while. The whole tone here just feels different now. Lately, it's seeming like it's more about results and money than anything or anyone else. I'm the first one to get business metrics, believe me. But when our culture principles say employees are the most important asset and yet my reality is completely different, well that's a problem.*

Jessie: *Wow, I'm completely surprised, Tam. I wish I had seen this coming.*

Tam: *Me too.* <Fade to black>

Ouch. If you have ever been caught off guard by what felt like an abrupt departure of one of your top performers, you're not alone. Many people leaders from seasoned executives to new supervisors have unfortunately encountered one of those "I sure didn't see that one coming" moments.

There's a lot of uncertainty these days in determining what new factors are influencing employees' decisions to leave or stay. We're in a stage of redefining engagement rules and adapting work models accordingly. This is evident by the focus on what returning to work currently looks like for many companies. Is it on-site for everybody again? If so, do we risk losing the people who say no to that? Where possible, can remote working opportunities sway a decision to stay? Can we create the needed cohesiveness and team collaboration with one-third of the team working from home, one-third on-site, and the remaining one-third working a combination of both?

And there's a new wrinkle in the mix: these plans and new models are no longer being created behind HR doors in an organizational vacuum. Employees are asking for transparency, clarity, and a voice in the specific outcomes that will affect them.

Discovering the reasons employees leave can sometimes be as complex as the individuals are themselves. Yet, getting to the root source of the real drivers behind a decision to leave is made easier if we first know where to look. When a top performer says "I quit," it's typically not a random event that sprang out of nowhere but has more likely been in the making for weeks, months, maybe even years. Most leaders don't see it coming especially with a top performer. It can be easy to miss the warning signs, misread the symptoms, or mistakenly assume everything is fine, because top performers like Tam usually say it is. Until one day it's not fine and then it's too late.

PART I

WHAT GOT US HERE?

The pandemic has set off a change reaction in the workplace unlike anything we've seen before and poses the question, How did we get here and so quickly? This opening section begins with a brief historical overview of the working conditions from several decades ago and the resulting pent-up frustrations that have impacted employees' expectations in the workplace, resulting in the current "I quit" explosion. It also looks at the assessments companies have traditionally used such as employee engagement surveys, exit interviews, and stay interviews in the attempt to collect turnover data and design strategic initiatives in hopes of improving employee retention.

PANDEMIC: THE GREAT REVEALER

Blend one part pent-up frustrations with employers, add two parts of no control over the work environment, mix in a gallon of awareness that life is fragile, and a taste of flexibility from working at home. The result? An "I quit!" explosion.

The hard-hitting pandemic completely overturned the foundation of what some considered an age-old, rock-solid workplace to reveal an onslaught of scurrying critters hiding underneath. Like a piercing laser beam, the pandemic penetrated directly into the heart of every organization and its employees by triggering one of the most profound individual and organizational assessment periods in the history of work.

Companies perhaps for the first time were tested to see if the values and tenets they proclaimed to hold sacred in their mission statement actually held up with observable behaviors when under fire. Some organizations passed with flying colors, some crashed and burned, and many survived but were handed a whole new set of marching orders from the people who stayed.

As devastating as the pandemic has been for so many, it has also served as a catalyst to reveal many workplace changes that have been overdue for decades. We couldn't fix what we didn't know was broken, and we can no longer hide what we always knew wasn't working in the hopes it would change on its own for the better or erode in a dark corner somewhere. It's all about complete transparency now.

In addition to being a wake-up call for organizations, the pandemic has also become the Great Revealer for employees, especially top talent who, knowing their worth on the labor market, left their prior positions and are now carefully analyzing their next choices. Employees are self-reflecting and for the first time questioning what they ultimately want from life and how work will need to fit into that new life plan in the future. Instead of bringing their chihuahua to work, they want to bring their authentic self to work, be it on-site or remotely. Instead of free food, they want flexibility. Most importantly they want to feel respected and valued as a human being in exchange for any superficial attempt to entertain them.

Work, for so many in previous decades, was the primary source of identity and validation as a person. What someone did for a living was an integral part of their makeup, self-worth, and reputation. Such is not the case anymore. The entity of work as we know it today has been reduced by today's employees to just one of many tools available to them to forge a bigger life plan. Work is no longer the end-all or be-all to the new definition of a successful life.

DANGER! EXPLOSIVES

Since the pandemic began, we've been watching a perfect storm play out before our eyes. Access any news stream to hear what you already know: the US Bureau of Labor Statistics and Job Openings Labor Turnover Surveys continue to report record-breaking quit rates, employee dissatisfaction, disengagement, unprecedented labor shortages, and resulting supply chain issues. Schools have been hard hit. Administrators who once culled through an abundance of qualified teaching applications have recently resorted to billboard messaging that says, "Want to teach? When can you start?"

Add to that, a lack of school bus drivers prompting districts to pay parents for driving their own kids to school. In some industries employees, who are so quickly suffering burnout from dealing with disgruntled customers (hospitality industry) or trying to care for others (healthcare) while putting their own needs aside just to keep pace on the job, are walking out on a moment's notice.

Why did this happen and so quickly? What was the fury behind the intensity and speed to which people literally walked off the job?

Let's begin by first pondering another question: What can happen if you mix two incompatible chemical agents together? Answer: an explosion. And that's exactly what we got—an "I quit!" explosion. When you mix decades of employees' pent-up frustrations from working in an employer-centric world with no control, add a keg of instant pontification on the possibility that life can end in the blink of an eye, and sprinkle in a little accelerator of experiencing benefits of working from home and poof! An explosive chorus erupted around the world singing a variation of "Take this job and shove it!"

The best news about the "I quit" explosion is that a period of reckoning has been born out of it and will continue to get bigger and stronger in the years to come. It's all valuable if we learn from the past and use those lessons to set up a better course of action for the future.

IMPACT ON TOP PERFORMERS

The pandemic has certainly resulted in many employees leaving, which in and of itself is challenging for any type of business to maintain their status quo let alone grow. But if any of those employees happen to be your top performers, the ramifications go even further. Which is why it's all the more urgent to care for the ones you still have.

Most people leaders readily know who their top performers are, but sometimes it may not be as clear at the onset. Some top performers are not in the limelight with the most advanced degrees, knowledge, or experience. More importantly, they are recognized by their work ethic, attitudes, and desire to get results as shown by the following traits:

- **The scope of their role is beyond their immediate job.** You will rarely hear "that's not my job" from a top performer. The bigger picture is their job, and they take the initiative to go above and beyond without needing to be asked. They don't wait to be told what to do; instead, they look to see what needs to be done.

- **They are goal oriented.** Top performers always have their eye on the finish line and accomplishments. They are driven to complete tasks regardless of obstacles. When situations get tough, they take ownership instead of placing blame. They don't care about clocking hours; instead, they aim to get results by doing whatever it takes.

- **They see change as a growth opportunity.** Instead of change being annoying, unfair, or a threat to their safety, top performers see change as a way to refocus their efforts, supercharge their skills, and take on a new target. They thrive on innovation and continuous growth.

- **They are culture stabilizers.** Top performers don't fuel drama; they have a high degree of emotional intelligence and are able to easily navigate around politics and chaos rather than getting sucked into it. They are too busy delivering results for the business and achieving personal goals. As a result, their presence on a team promotes a positive and collaborative culture.

Top performers also have a strong proclivity toward overt and covert leadership, which, when it comes to employee retention, can have a positive or negative impact on other team members. Coworkers are also typically aware who the top performers are. They watch and see their positive influence on the team when they are selected for key assignments and win special recognition rewards. Other employees who want to progress look to them as the unspoken role models for how to behave and the silent weather vanes who know which way the wind is blowing and demonstrate the authentic culture of the business by the way leadership treats them.

When a top performer quits, it's more than your business potential and competitive knowledge base that walks out the door. Their leaving creates a vacuum for others to follow suit. Their action sets off a firestorm where employees are more likely to reevaluate their entire relationship with the company. Thoughts of, "If this is the way the superstar gets treated, what are my chances here?" will ripple throughout the ranks and validate others who may be contemplating leaving to act upon that decision once the top performer exits.

The loss of solid performers can be crippling to an organization's morale and validates the belief that quitting is the only natural choice. Those employees who remain will internalize the loss of the top performer by the impact on their existing workload. If they are already harboring seeds of dissatisfaction, that may be just the catalyst to exit before the additional work is piled on.

Those top performers who did leave their previous employers and are looking to land a new opportunity are also scrutinizing how companies treated their employees during the pandemic. Companies who put their employees first by providing some sort of emergency benefits, care for their physical and emotional safety, or financially assisted those furloughed are the ones candidates are now seeking for employment. While processes and profits will always be critical for business success, the message is getting louder and clearer that the care and retention of the people driving those processes and profits has now taken center stage.

CHANGE WITH A CAPITAL C

The Greek philosopher Heraclitus once said, "Change is the only constant in life." Anybody who's been in the workplace for even a short period of time would certainly know that to be true. There has been so much constant change in the workplace over the past decades that the term *change fatigue* has recently become one of the characteristics to describe employee burnout.

Most previous workplace changes have been a result of advancing technology, improved logistics, or pursuit of operational efficiencies through the use of better tools and resources. What makes this workplace shift so different is that for the first time it's not about extrinsic forces like technology, tools, or resources; rather, it's about behavior changes—personal, intrinsic drives within the very people doing the work. This is what has made this particular change such a big one and so challenging to work through.

Changes that bring solutions and systems improvements with minimal disruption to status quo work models are easier to implement. Depending on the nature of the change, they are either enthusiastically accepted or at least slowly adapted over time by those they impact.

An example of enthusiastic acceptance to change was seen in the early 1960s when the new owners of a credit data reporting agency made what was considered to be a major process improvement at the time. The goal was to decrease the number of minutes it took a service agent to answer an inquiry call from a credit provider wanting to know a potential customer's credit rating.

When the call came in, the agent had to leave their station, walk to a wall of drawers twenty feet away, access the filed 3x5 card with the data needed, walk back to the phone, relay the information, complete the call, get back up, go back to the file, replace the card, walk back to their desk, and take the next call.

The whole process took an average of twelve minutes with the ability to handle about five calls per hour. That major process improvement happened when the owners had ball-bearing wheels installed on the agents' chairs allowing them to stay seated, push off and wheel over to the card wall and back, resulting in shaving an average of four minutes off each call. The agents loved it, productivity soared (literally), the working model wasn't disrupted (important fact), and everything just got better and faster.

While this story may be an amusing ditty about productivity and change, the point is as with most operational improvements in the workplace prior to the pandemic, it happened at an emotionally safe distance for those it impacted and for the organization implementing it. The changes in the workplace as a result of the pandemic, however, did not occur at an emotionally safe distance. These changes crossed over the personal boundaries of almost every person in the workplace by taking root in their homes, invading personal spaces, impacting family dynamics, and threatening levels of emotional and psychological safety that have not been impacted before on such a broad level. When the basic human needs of a person are in jeopardy, the response is usually not a mild one.

TAKE FIVE

1. Employees in the new workplace expect transparency from their leader as well as from the organization. They want honest dialogue and an opportunity to share their voice.

2. The pandemic has been a positive catalyst for workplace change and reassessment. Use it to look within at the team and the organization to see what can be made better.

3. Employees want to feel respected and valued as a human beings in exchange for any superficial attempt to entertain them.

4. The "I quit" explosion resulted from mixing a volatile concoction of pent-up frustrations with employers, plus no control over the work environment, an awareness that life is fragile, and a taste of flexibility from working at home.

5. The changes in the workplace as a result of the pandemic did not occur at an emotionally safe distance, differentiating them from all other workplace changes in the past.

At the end of each chapter you will find Survival Tactics designed to help you immediately put the main concepts into action. I urge you to act upon these activities, complete the team worksheets, use the checklists, and evaluate yourself. There are no right or wrong answers, just practical steps for you to implement what you will learn and valuable insights for your team and organization. Exclusively for readers of this book: Download a user-friendly copy of the Big Quit Survival Kit that contains all the Survival Tactics in a printable 8½ x 11–size format. Go to www.BigQuitSurvivalGuide.com, click on the *Download Survival Kit* tab and enter the password: survival.

SURVIVAL TACTIC #1
PANDEMIC IMPACT QUESTIONNAIRE

Reflecting on the recent changes and new strategies will help build resilience going forward.

1. What has been the biggest challenge for your company to overcome since the pandemic?

2. What have you learned as a result?

3. If you had a crystal ball in 2020 and knew the pandemic was on the horizon, what would you as a people leader or business owner have done differently?

4. How has your team and organizational culture changed as a result?

5. Employees are asking to be treated as human beings. What does that mean for the people you are leading? What would they like you to continue doing, start doing, or stop doing as a result?

6. What positive outcomes has the pandemic brought to you as a person and to the company? How are you a better leader as a result? How is the company stronger?

7. What are some of the innovations and new growth opportunities the pandemic has opened for you and the business?

8. What business trends as a result of the pandemic do you see continuing that will impact your business?

9. How are you planning to stay current and be ready to meet these trends?

10. What is the one accomplishment you are proudest of as you have come through the pandemic? What will you do to ensure that accomplishment will continue in the future?

SURVIVAL TACTIC #2
TOP PERFORMER INVENTORY

The first step in retaining your top performers is to recognize who they are and how they are contributing to your team. Review the traits of top performers and note who on your team is displaying any or all of the traits and in what way.

Top performer traits

- Scope of their role is beyond their immediate job

- Goal oriented

- See change as a growth opportunity

- Culture stabilizers

TEAM MEMBER	TRAITS	OBSERVED ACTIONS/BEHAVIORS

SURVIVAL TACTIC #3
NAME IT AND CLAIM IT TEAM DISCUSSION

In addition to wanting to be treated like a human being, employees are expecting transparency and authenticity. Those are abstract words and need to be defined by the people asking for them. Hold a team discussion to get clarity on what *transparency* looks like so you can target your behaviors as the leader and hold the team accountable for theirs.

1. Introduce the discussion: *We all want to ensure that working together is as caring and respectful as possible, and we hear a lot about being transparent with each other. Let's drill down on what exactly that means, so we are demonstrating transparent behaviors with each other. Let's start by defining what transparency looks like.*

2. If the meeting is in person, hand out a 3x5 index card to each team member and have them write "transparency" at the top followed by their definition. If team members are remote, they can annotate on a whiteboard or post their definition on a message board.

3. Next, collect everyone's cards, read them aloud, and capture their thoughts on an easel board or whiteboard so everyone can see the collective definitions. Note what themes are emerging such as being honest, being accessible, or trusting—and highlight the two to three most common.

4. Share what specific behaviors and actions you will commit to as the leader to embody the team's collective definition of transparency.

5. Ask each team member to share a specific action or behavior they will adopt to demonstrate transparency with each other.

Note: This exercise can be repeated with any abstract words such as *being authentic, treated like a human being, trust, respectful,* among others.

2

HOW WORK GOT DONE:
THE GREAT PRESSURE COOKER

Up until now employees had a job, not a voice.

Years of pent-up frustrations by employees feeling they had little if any say in what has traditionally been an employer-controlled environment for most of the past fifty years set off the "I quit" explosion. It's worth taking a minute to look back and understand where these frustrations came from and why they kept building to avoid unconsciously creating a new batch in the future.

Beginning with the post–World War II economic boom, the manufacturing industry was on a competitive mission to produce as much product as quickly as possible. The country was turning out record numbers of new cars, televisions, and consumer goods at an unstoppable pace. The invention of the assembly line, attributed to Henry Ford, sped up the workflow even faster as larger and more complex assembly processes were broken into smaller, independent tasks requiring lower skilled workers and lower wages.

Along with the increase of mass production workers came the demand for supervisors to manage them. We can all recall Lucy and Ethel's madcap frenzy of trying to wrap candy pieces speeding toward them on a conveyor belt as a supervisor barked orders and cranked up the speed as their sole reward for keeping pace.

For decades employees worked under a command and control approach. They didn't question policies, raise concerns, or complain about long hours, out of fear of getting fired. Henry Ford was one of the early adopters of a more humanistic approach to leadership. In considering ways to attract and retain top talent, he shortened the typical ten- to twelve-hour day to an eight-hour day with paid breaks— the same model still in place throughout many industries today.

He also knew that assembly workers on the front lines needed a higher sense of purpose in what they did all day, and he hung large posters on the factory walls that displayed happy customers with thank-you notes for the quality and craftsmanship of their new cars, thus creating a sense of higher purpose and engagement than just connecting a thousand widget As and widget Bs all day.

In addition to assembly line employees, office pool workers sitting at tightly packed rows of desks inspired by factory layouts found themselves subjected to a similar type of command and control. They kept their heads down and eyes on their work. Breaks were by request only. The constant noise level of clanging typewriters and clicking adding machines was deafening, and cigarette smoke was prevalent throughout the long workday.

Employee retention in those days was driven more by fear than loyalty. It wasn't until union activities in the late 1970s did workplaces begin to make the connection that satisfied employees were more likely to create satisfied customers. Employee benefits and welfare programs started to surface, and new leadership principles such as management by walking around were adopted by supervisors as a way to get to know their employees and motivate them using a more humanistic approach.

MAYBE IS THE NEW LOYALTY

When people joined an organization in the previous decades, they expected to stay with that firm for a lifetime. There was an unspoken expectation among employees that if they did an acceptable job, the company would take care of them for their working lifetime, and for many that was exactly the case. Job hopping was looked upon as something negative, viewed by interviewers as an "unsteady" characteristic and thus raising concerns for a candidate's potential stability.

Unlike today, employees didn't have exposure to social media sites where hundreds of jobs were in the wings to replace their current one, and top talent didn't receive daily emails from recruiters enticing them away with bigger and better opportunities. So employees silently stayed despite a burning desire to leave conditions they despised and a boss they detested.

Up until the pandemic, the Great Recession of the late 2000s was the most recent watershed event to impact the workplace. That unspoken loyalty bond between employer and employee quickly vanished overnight along with many 401(k)s. Millennials thinking about entering the workplace took note that there were no guarantees when it came to employment, even after twenty years of a commitment like many saw their parents make.

The message of "take care of yourself because nobody else will" had a strong influence in the way they thought about work. As a result, they replaced the employer-employee loyalty commitment with that of a contractual business transaction. "If you do this for me, I will do that for you" became their condition for seeking employment, and for the first time employees rather than employers had the upper hand.

Top performers have added an extra element to this conditional transaction that says, "and by the way, I will stay with you as long as I am building my market value." Top performers know their worth on the street and are leveraging it. One of the best ways to keep them is to ensure they are acquiring new skills and have access to the training and experiences that will support the continued growth of their own human capital.

While the pent-up reasons that helped ignite the "I quit" explosion may not be referred to as command and control today, we can recognize the same feelings being expressed in more familiar terms like *micromanaged, inflexible, excluded, disrespected, unfulfilled,* and *undervalued.* Employees didn't quit their job as much as they quit the feelings they got from doing their job.

Organizations now have a window of opportunity to retool their employee processes to align with the expectations of those they want to attract and keep. Employees have made it easier by removing most of the guesswork regarding expectations. Top performers want to align with leaders and organizations who welcome diverse opinions and are open to healthy and respectful dialogues on different ways of thinking. They are joining those companies that value bringing new ideas into the open and understand that conflict resolution and community problem solving are the desired avenues to growth on all fronts. Organizations will do well to springboard that information as a starting point.

TAKE FIVE

1. For decades employees worked under a command and control management approach, which, when combined with an acute awareness that life is fragile, and the opportunity to work remotely with more flexibility, released a pent-up decision to leave a job that no longer emotionally supported them.

2. A turning point for how millennials viewed the workplace was the layoffs during the Great Recession and the realization of no long-term employment guarantees.

3. Employee loyalty has given way to a transactional business relationship with their employer, as in, "If you do this for me, I will do this for you."

4. Top performers also require ongoing investment in their marketability through upskilling, training, and growth opportunities.

5. The "I quit" explosion resulted from mixing employees' pent-up frustrations of having no control over their work environment with an awareness that life is fragile and a taste of flexibility with working remotely.

SURVIVAL TACTIC
SHARE LUCY AND THE CHOCOLATE FACTORY

Show your team the three-minute YouTube clip, Lucy and the Chocolate Factory, and share a brief discussion around the following questions. Bring in a box of chocolates to share for some extra ambiance and fun. Make sure to send a treat to your remote team members too.

1. What do you think it was like working for a business fifty years ago? Do you have any stories your relatives may have shared?

2. How has work changed since then?

3. In what ways has it stayed the same?

4. In what ways can your job feel like working in a pressure cooker here?

5. What do we need to be mindful of as a result? How can we make work better?

3

THE ELUSIVE PURSUIT OF EMPLOYEE ENGAGEMENT

Engaged employees are created one person at a time.

The last couple of decades have brought pervasive opportunities to work remotely, and as a result employees' work lives and personal lives continue to meld into one. It used to be that people compartmentalized those two worlds and derived a main source of pleasure from personal activities once their work was completed for the day. There was ample opportunity for enjoying family time and hobbies. But a blurring of the work and personal worlds has shifted to where, now, employees are looking to their jobs as an integral part of their desire for fulfillment.

Work has crossed into the feelings zone. How someone feels about their job is proving to have a major impact on their decision to stay in it. Going to work for the simple reward of a paycheck is being replaced by the desire to be respected, which puts a whole new twist on the ability to measure employee engagement. When people are made to feel cared for, those feelings drive commitment and loyalty just like that of a personal relationship.

In addition to the impact of the pandemic, and employees' frustrations with prolonged feelings of no control over their work environment, a third consideration regarding the topic of this part of the book—What Got Us Here?—is the ineffectiveness of employee engagement assessments to determine the root causes of turnover within a particular organization.

The term *employee engagement* came into being in the early 1990s. William A. Kahn, in his paper, "Psychological Conditions of Personal Engagement and Disengagement at Work," published in the *Academy of Management Journal*, described the psychological, emotional, and physical conditions necessary for people to feel engaged or disengaged at work. His research focused on a sense of self that employees attached to their work role as an outlet to express a significant portion of their identity. When the aspects of the work align to a positive sense of self, engagement was the outcome. When the sense of self is conflicted with the work being done, disengagement is the result.

ENGAGEMENT SURVEYS ARE COMING UP SHORT

Since the 1990s companies have used many types of assessments. The intent is to measure the degree of positivity employees are feeling about their jobs and the organization as a whole. Depending on their size and scope, engagement surveys can be expensive to administrate and analyze and time consuming to execute follow-up action items. The data are sometimes used to glean any potential indicators of employee retention, but despite the evolution and sophistication of these surveys, there is a widening conclusion that their effectiveness is far from exceeding expectations.

Forbes conducted a recent survey of human resource leaders where 78% said they are failing to get desired results from employee engagement surveys. There appear to be several inherent reasons as to why:

- Lack of trust in the anonymity of responses potentially skews responses to the positive.

- The survey's availability window of two to three weeks, every one to two years is too narrow to apply generalizations.

- People report on biased feelings based on short-term positive or negative experiences.

- Too broad of an attempt to boil the ocean resulting in little or no measurable impact in one area.

- Lack of personalized employee action plans. Retention initiatives are too generalized and don't get to the roots of dissatisfaction at the individual employee level, which matters most.

EXIT INTERVIEWS: TOO LITTLE, WAY TOO LATE

In addition to employee engagement surveys, some companies also use exit interviews in the attempt to identify the deeper reasons behind someone's decision to leave, especially when that someone is one of the most highly valued employees in the organization. Companies earnestly want to know what they needed to have done differently to have changed the employee's decision. Note the number of past tenses used in the previous sentence, which reveals one of the inherent problems with exit interviews: they provide little information, way too late.

Typically, a top performer's decision to leave was not done on a whim or spur of the moment. The conditions and experiences that brought them to their exit decision were likely building over time when their leader should have been aware of the changing circumstances creating the dissatisfaction and proactively addressed them. Once an employee has made the decision to leave, the use of standard exit interview questions provides little ability for the company to salvage the loss. Imagine a top performer who has already resigned, being asked these meaningless questions:

- When did you start looking for another job?

- Why were you looking for a new job?

- Did you feel that you were equipped to do your job here?

- How did the culture impact your decision to leave?

- Were you satisfied with the way you were managed?

- What could we have done to change your decision to leave?

Because top performers aren't notorious for burning professional bridges, they will also refrain from making any disparaging remarks about a previous boss or employer and prefer to stay focused on the positive opportunity that came their way as opposed to any negative circumstances triggering the desire to leave. Sometimes you may get worthwhile feedback that can actually be implemented, but many exiting employees will just professionally thank you for the experience and stand on the fact that they couldn't turn down a fantastic opportunity that serendipitously came along as the perfect job fit for what they needed in life at that exact moment. (Truth be told, they were proactively searching for that fortuitous opportunity for months.)

At times, exit interviews may result in the opposite effect with employees who merely have an ax to grind and can offer nothing more than dumping a giant gunny sack filled with every cataloged injustice, issue, and accusation dating back from employment day one, leaving the poor interviewer more dazed than enlightened. Either way, exit interviews are not the best tools for collecting usable retention data.

STAY INTERVIEWS: GETTING WARMER

When compared with engagement surveys and exit interviews, stay interviews are closer to a better option for a general read on an employee's job satisfaction level. They tend to be around twenty to thirty minutes and are done more casually and frequently. Some leaders like to rotate the questions into 1:1 meetings or use as a monthly stand-alone check-in.

Stay interview questions may include topics like these:

- What are your thoughts as you start a new workweek?

- What do you look forward to each day on the job?

- What do you like most about working here?

- How do you currently rate your work-life balance? Why?

- What does your dream job look like? How does your current job compare?

- What would you change about your current job if you could?

Stay interview questions tend to prompt a deeper conversation about the employee's feelings, and their frequency provides a timelier collection of information than the annual or semiannual engagement survey. When compared with exit interviews, they are more strategically positioned to drive information that may help to get a read on retention. In both cases, however, the questions still tend to be too general to get to real issues that drive a decision to stay or uncover any issues that may be pushing an employee to think about leaving.

Asking a top-performing programmer to describe their dream job and getting a reply of race car driver or drummer in a rock band may provide interesting background knowledge, but what exactly does one do with that information from a retention standpoint? There is still a need to get to a deeper level of what an employee is feeling and experiencing while doing the job in order to determine whether they want to keep doing it or not.

ENGAGED EMPLOYEES ARE CREATED ONE PERSON AT A TIME

The ability to act on potential turnover data collected by employee engagement surveys, exit interviews, and stay interviews can be challenging. The information even distilled down to the department or team level is still too generalized to have a meaningful effect on individual employees. Retention solutions based on macro-level trends instead of clarifying the micro-level needs of each employee are not effective avenues to address reasons for turnover. In other words, employee retention is a person-by-person issue that cannot be initially addressed with an organizational, one-size-fits-all approach.

We've seen multiple examples of attempts over the years to offer all kinds of untargeted perks and programs in the hopes of retaining the best people. Everything, you name it, has been tried from free food and drinks, Ping-Pong tables, dartboards, redesigned compensation plans, relaxed dress codes, redesigned offices, nap rooms, yoga rooms, gym rooms, safe rooms, on-site massages, errand services, bring your pet to work, bring your kid to work, time off to volunteer, work from home, (pre-pandemic) flexible scheduling, more training, open environments, open teams, open projects, open feedback, private feedback, peer feedback, no feedback, fix the culture, fix the leader, fix the tools, fix the processes, and on and on it goes. An endless cycle of spending money and resources to keep the employees happy, engaged, and fulfilled and all with less than stellar results.

What we have learned since then despite all the best company efforts is the one conclusion that bears repeating: employee retention is first an *individual* problem that cannot be directly solved with an *organizational* solution.

UP CLOSE, IT IS PERSONAL

Picture the people in your organization as a digitized image, like a wall-sized poster of the Statue of Liberty hanging in a storefront window. From across the street, you see a beautiful capture of that famous landmark. However, as you move closer to further inspect it, it's evident that's not a photo of the Statue of Liberty itself but rather thousands of tiny digitized portraits of people's faces that when combined make up the portrayal of the statue. Observing the poster as only an excellent rendering of the Statue of Liberty is a surface response. It completely misses the fact that individual, unique, digitized faces create the total image.

Too often, an organization uses the same type of surface vision when trying to understand their turnover issue and misses the fact that the bigger picture is made up of tiny, individual pixels instead. They view an employee retention issue as a large-scale rendering hovering over the organization and mistakenly aim at surface attempts to fix it.

Leaders need to get up close and personal to see the pixels of each of their employees they want to retain and address any dissatisfaction issues at that micro level instead. The quickest way to build a productive business of motivated, engaged, and happy top performers who want to stay is with one individual employee at a time. Unfortunately, there are no shortcuts.

EMPLOYEE RETENTION DATA THAT MATTER: THE 3-R CONVERSATION

While engagement surveys may be helpful to determine employee opinions on the quality of benefits, accessibility to training, or equitable pay, the research continues to prove they are not the best providers of actionable retention data. The heart of uncovering why someone elects to leave or stay is an individual issue. Therefore, the best way to collect employee retention data that matter would be to ask one employee at a time.

You may be thinking, yes, got that already, but asking them what exactly? To best answer that, let's go back to the concept of balancing that 3-R scale initially introduced in the opening section of this book and to be developed even more in coming chapters. If you recall, people are already formulating their own engagement questions as a way to internalize their ongoing decision to leave or stay with the organization.

- What is it costing me physically and psychologically to succeed at this job? (Requirements)

- What am I tangibly getting in return for doing this job? (Rewards)

- How appreciated, trusted, and valued do I feel on this job? (Respect)

An employee's collective answers will result in either a balance or imbalance in their perceptions of what they are expected to do when compared with what they are getting in return. If the Requirements balance with the Rewards and Respect, they will likely decide to stay. If not, they may start thinking it's not worth it and begin heading toward the door unless the scale is calibrated back into balance.

It should start to make sense, then, that one of the most effective ways a people leader can get a true read on their employee's engagement level would be to consistently have conversations that center on the same questions employees are already asking themselves. These are called 3-R conversations as they address the Requirements, Rewards, and Respect the employee is continuously assessing to determine whether they will leave or stay.

A 3-R conversation between a people leader and their individual team member focuses on one primary theme: the ongoing balance an employee is feeling between fulfilling the Requirements of the job with the Rewards and Respect they're getting in return. There's an added bonus to having regular 3-R conversations with your employees. Not only will you start to get to the level of questions necessary to help assess engagement and retention, but you will also be providing what employees say is the most important thing they want from an employer right now, and that's to simply be treated as a human being.

In 3-R conversations the questions and tone center on employees as unique individuals and focus on them as a holistic person, not as a cog in the organizational wheel or line on an org chart.

Every employee has their own set of personalized values. Values place different weights on the Requirements needed to succeed at a job and ultimately guide employees in their decision to leave or stay.

As appropriate, talk with your employee and seek to understand if the values they hold line up with the job they are performing. By investing the time to learn what each top performer values, what they define as most motivating, and identifying anything that is getting in their way, people leaders can more effectively personalize each top performer's employment journey so that it's a joint win for both the organization and the employee.

Such an approach will certainly help create a clearer path of what's needed to keep them. The real magic of employee engagement begins with the people leader's willingness to first connect with each employee as a unique human being, which is exactly what employees are asking for right now.

TAKE FIVE

1. Companies have used employee engagement surveys with little success in the ability to map causes and solutions to employee turnover issues.

2. Because they typically don't burn bridges, top performers tend not to be forthcoming when asked reasons for leaving in an exit interview. Also, the process is too late to intervene after the decision to leave has been made.

3. Stay interviews, while better options, tend to be too generalized and the questions not targeted enough to uncover potential turnover issues.

4. The most effective way to understand an individual's mindset about job satisfaction is to have ongoing 3-R conversations that focus on the balance of their current state of the Requirements necessary to succeed at the job and the Rewards and Respect levels being received in return.

5. Every employee has their own set of personalized values. Values place different weights on the Requirements needed to succeed at a job and ultimately guide employees in their decision to leave or stay.

SURVIVAL TACTIC #1
VALUES CLARIFICATION EXERCISE

Employees today want a sense of meaning and purpose from the work they are doing. To understand how these drivers are impacting the engagement of your employees, the first step is to define what each of them values. Send this Values Clarification Exercise to the team and share the results with the group. Be sure to include yourself.

1. Cross off any values NOT IMPORTANT.

2. Circle those values that are MOST IMPORTANT. Add any that are missing for you.

3. From your MOST IMPORTANT values, rank order your top five.

Accountability	Diversity	Independence	Productivity
Achievement	Effectiveness Responsibility	Influencing	Quality
Advancement	Environmental	Innovation	Recognition
Adventure	Equality	Integrity	Relationships
Arts	Excellence	Intellectualism	Responsibility
Autonomy	Excitement	Involvement	Security
Beauty	Expertise	Knowledge	Self-awareness
Belonging	Fairness	Leadership	Self-respect
Challenge	Fame	Learning	Self-realization
Change	Family	Mastery	Serenity
Collaboration	Financial Gain	Meaningful Work	Sophistication
Communication	Freedom	Merit	Spirituality
Community	Friendship	Nature	Stability
Competence	Fun	Openness	Status
Competition	Harmony	Order	Structure
Cooperation	Health	Personal	Teamwork
Creativity	Helping Others	Pleasure	Truth
Curiosity	Helping Society	Power	Variety
Decisiveness	Honesty	Prestige	
Democracy	Humor	Privacy	

SURVIVAL TACTIC #2
VALUES ENGAGEMENT INVENTORY

MY TOP 5 VALUES	WAYS I DEMONSTRATE THIS VALUE AT WORK
1.	
2.	
3.	
4.	
5.	

After the team completes the Values Clarification Exercise, capture the information for your top performers and fill in the following grid:

PERFORMER	5 TOP VALUES	INDICATORS OF ENGAGEMENT AND FULFILLMENT

PART II

GOING MENTAL: THE PSYCHOLOGY OF WORK

People are people, *first*. That's the foundation behind why employees are asking their employers to treat them as human beings.

All people have basic human needs despite differences in gender identity, age, race, demographics, location, education, titles, status, or wealth. While there are some generational nuances, people's basic human needs will always remain constant. By understanding these needs and a bit of motivation theory, you will see how these forces are reshaping the work environments that employees are willing to join.

In this section, burnout is also extensively discussed as a byproduct of work and the primary reason why millions of people have left their jobs in recent months. Burnout is definitely on the rise. For the first time we are seeing it impact top performers and people leaders in a major way as they not only try to work through their own mental wellness issues but are tasked to care for the mental well-being of their team members as well—all with little or no training on how to do so. Behavioral warning lights of potential burnout are also noted in this section to help alert people leaders on what to watch for and how to take preventive steps as recommended.

PEOPLE ARE *PEOPLE*, FIRST: BASIC NEEDS AND MOTIVATORS

Please, just treat me as a human being.

The relationship between people and work goes back to the first humans' need for survival. Their daily food requirement and need for protective shelter prompted three of the most important job postings of their day: hunter, gatherer, and builder.

In today's work environment, because food and shelter are more readily available than they were for our ancestors, the basic need to work has shifted from that of survival to the higher need for self-actualization and the pursuit of fulfilling one's maximum potential. Even though we still essentially work for food and shelter, we are far removed from the basic survival motivators that drove our ancestors to work.

If the Great Resignation has surfaced anything, it has emphasized a shift in how employees are defining their purpose not just at work but in life. They are looking for work that provides a stronger sense of fulfillment and will be more inclined to stay in an environment where their work is contributing to that bigger purpose they want out of life.

GETTING DOWN TO BASICS

An extremely successful global business leader was once quoted as saying, "Take my best twenty people and there goes my businesses." If the success of a people leader is contingent on the success of their team and that team's overall success is dependent on the performance of each person, it makes sense then for the leader to focus on each individual and identify the basic needs and motivators for the ones they wish to keep.

Every human being carries around an invisible suitcase throughout their workday that contains their basic needs, as psychologist Abraham Maslow acknowledged. The most basic of these needs are physiological like air, food, water, and sleep to keep us functional. The additional needs for security, safety, love, belonging, self-esteem, and self-actualization, and the desire to fulfill our ultimate potential, fill the rest of that suitcase and are the rudimentary drivers behind all people's actions and behaviors.

These fundamental human needs are sometimes so powerful that people will do whatever it takes to meet them, either positively or negatively. If the need for love and belonging is not met in a healthy and socially acceptable way, the relentless drive will continue even at the expense of the person's ultimate welfare as in joining a gang or cult or staying in an abusive relationship.

People leaders who have educated themselves in the study of human needs and motivation theories or who just have a natural interest in psychology do well in their ability to understand and relate to their individual team members. However, most business leaders receive little if any formal leadership training on how to execute the tactical components of their job, let alone understand the psychological dynamics that dictate the behaviors of the people they're leading.

The most unfortunate aspect of that reality is that leaders are missing out on the capability to master the basics of what ultimately drives human behavior. When the human aspect is cared for, it is eye-opening to see the degree to which employees flourish and can accomplish their goals with a high level of ongoing job satisfaction and engagement. Going forward, as the employees' cry of "treat me as a human being" continues to get louder, it is hopeful that people leaders will receive training in this critical area to better understand and motivate the people they are leading.

WHY SOME WORK HARDER

Beginning in the early 1950s, psychologist Frederick Herzberg explored what drove employee satisfaction. He wanted to learn why some people worked harder than others, so he asked employees to describe those situations when they felt exceptionally satisfied about their job and when they felt exceptionally dissatisfied. His findings revealed that the aspects of a job attributed to satisfaction were distinctively different from those that generated dissatisfaction. As a result, he presented what he called the two-factor theory consisting of motivating and hygiene factors.

Herzberg labeled the causes of job satisfaction as motivating factors. They included intrinsic characteristics such as achievement, opportunity to do meaningful work, responsibility, growth, and involvement in decision-making. Additionally, he labeled those causes that contributed to job dissatisfaction as hygiene factors or maintenance factors extrinsic to the work itself. They represented more of the tangibles offered in return for the work completed. These included a paycheck, raises, job security, working conditions, company policies, health insurance, and paid time off. In themselves, the presence of hygiene factors did not contribute to increased job satisfaction or lead to higher motivation. Still, the absence of them could potentially result in dissatisfaction as in the case of fair compensation.

Money is not necessarily a motivator to work harder, but the absence of the amount of money needed to feel safe will result in dissatisfaction and lack of engagement in the desired intensity of work.

The absence of these hygiene factors can result in an underlying resentment among employees that if not carefully watched can be missed. An example is having flavored coffee pods in the breakroom one day and never replenishing them or spending money on a state-of-the-art hockey table game when customer service reps just wanted headphones that didn't keep cutting out.

Herzberg concluded that satisfaction and dissatisfaction factors are not on a continuum with one increasing as the other diminishes but are mutually exclusive, meaning that leaders need to acknowledge that they are different and to keep tabs on both equally.

NEVER WORK A DAY IN YOUR LIFE

Mark Twain is quoted as saying, "Find a job you enjoy doing and you will never have to work a day in your life." Employees who have a keen sense of purpose are the ones who look forward to the start of a new workweek as a way to reap the intrinsic rewards of self-fulfillment in the work they do. Successful people leaders know this and create ways to empower their teams with a vision of the higher purpose of their work.

As previously discussed, Henry Ford understood this concept and posted happy customer photos with their thank-you notes on factory walls as a way to help mitigate the monotony of standing on an assembly line day after day. He constantly reminded his workers what they were ultimately there to do: to positively impact people's lives with a beautiful, safe, and well-built vehicle.

Daniel Pink, in his book, *Drive: The Surprising Truth About What Motivates Us*, further supports this human approach to motivation and fulfillment by referencing the word *purpose* as the way employees will unlock their highest motivation level for doing work.

There's an old story about a bystander who approached a construction site where three people were laying bricks. Upon asking the first worker, "What are you doing?" the response was, "What does it look like? I'm laying bricks." The second worker replied to the same question with, "I am building a wall." And the third worker replied with resounding enthusiasm, "I am creating a magnificent cathedral!" Three people doing the same job, three completely different perspectives.

One of the organizations I have the privilege of working with does an excellent job of creating and sustaining a vision of a higher purpose for its employees, company-wide. Each morning people leaders kick off the day with their team by sharing the Daily Huddle. It's a brief document that features an employee who models the values of the organization while on the job. Each daily story reminds everyone of the higher purposes they have been called to fulfill and how their work individually contributes to that purpose.

ARE YOU LEADING ON PURPOSE?

What about the team you are leading? For example, as a restaurant owner, if a bystander were to ask any of your team members, "What are you doing?" which response would you like to hear? "I'm serving food" or "I'm delighting customers with a wonderful experience they can remember." As an elementary school principal, "I'm teaching kids to read" or "I'm in the process of giving a child the key to a successful life." Running a delivery service, "I drop off packages" or "I'm making sure a special birthday gift arrives on time." You get the picture.

Some employees are able to create their own vision of purpose while others need the help of a visionary people leader. Here are a few ways to start leading on purpose:

- **Start with yourself.** The team will see themselves as you do. Under your leadership are they laying bricks or creating cathedrals?

- **Create a draft of your own team purpose statement.** Begin the statement by answering these questions: Why does the team exist? What are the critical activities we perform? What do we want to be in the future? How will we get there? Invite the team to contribute and edit the document so that it becomes the reflection of what they aspire to be. Refer to it regularly as a reminder of what everyone is ultimately aiming to achieve.

- **Make it personal.** Where possible, provide positive feedback from customers, both internal and external. Share tangible examples of how someone's life has been made better as a result of their work. Post positive customer feedback on the team share site, or in the office. Add an inspirational quote to meeting agendas and kick off the meeting with a brief discussion on how the quote applies to the team's work.

- **Make it a routine.** Don't just try a one-and-done event to create feelings of a higher purpose. It's better if you don't do anything than make a lukewarm attempt and drop it. Like the Daily Huddle, incorporate the higher purpose of what you do each day, so the team lives it as part of their ongoing culture.

- **Reward behaviors in the context of the higher purpose.** If an employee has an exceptional month, not only acknowledge and reward their hard work but celebrate what that hard work meant for the higher purpose of the team's vision. While Sue can be rewarded for scheduling a record number of neighborhood baby wellness checks, the team can celebrate the fact that a record number of babies that month are going to get the preventive care they seriously need.

Employees in the new workplace have made it clear that they want a sense of purpose in the work they do and to ensure that the social values the company supports are in alignment with their own. It will be important for people leaders to stay aware of this need and help their teams to see how their work contributes to a higher purpose. Employees want to share goals and values with their employer and be able to contribute ideas and solutions.

TAKE FIVE

1. The foundation of how employees think and what will motivate them begins with the most basic of all sociological levelers, acknowledging that people are *people,* first. All people have basic human needs that take precedence over gender identity, age, race, demographics, location, education, titles, status, wealth, or generational differences.

2. Employees' basic needs for self-actualization are driving a sense to know that the work they are doing has meaning and they see the connection between what they do every day and how it contributes to the company and society in general. Without this sense of meaning, they will not be engaged.

3. Herzberg's two-factor model says that basic factors like safety and salary need to be met to prevent dissatisfaction at work, but that another set of higher order motivating factors like autonomy and recognition are required to create actual happiness at work.

4. The most effective people leaders help to provide a vision of a higher sense of purpose in their team as does self-reflecting on how they see the team's work. They create a team purpose statement and celebrate how the contributions of team members each serve the higher purpose of the team.

5. Employees want to share goals and values with their employer and be able to contribute ideas and solutions.

SURVIVAL TACTIC #1
ARE YOU LEADING ON PURPOSE?

Refer to the story of the three different bricklayers. Each one had a different perspective of doing the exact same activity. Employees want a sense of a higher calling and a meaningful purpose to what they are doing for work. Is your team doing nothing more than laying bricks or are they erecting a cathedral? How you view the work is the same way your people will.

Think about the work you are leading. Describe it in three levels. Level 1 is the most basic tactical description of what the team does. Level 2 is somewhat more visionary. Level 3 captures the higher calling. For example, if you lead a team in the computer department at a big box electronics store:

Level 1:   We sell computers.

Level 2:   We help people make the best choice for their unique online needs.

Level 3:   We empower people with ways to access information that matters most to them.

Your turn. What we do:

Level 1:

Level 2:

Level 3:

Create a draft of your own team purpose statement by answering these questions:

- Why does the team exist?

- What are the critical activities we perform?

- What do we want to be in the future?

- How will we get there?

Invite the team to contribute and edit the team purpose document so that it becomes the reflection of what they inspire to be. Refer to it regularly as a reminder of what everyone is ultimately aiming to achieve.

Keep the higher calling and team purpose visible:

- In what ways can you share tangible evidence of the impact the team is making in the lives of others?

- What can you do as a daily reminder of the higher calling of the team's purpose?

- In what ways are you recognizing and rewarding people on the team who demonstrate behaviors that support the team's higher calling and purpose?

SURVIVAL TACTIC #2
TEAM RALLY CRY OR SLOGAN

Create a team image or a rally cry that reflects the team's purpose. Start by asking the group to name three different adjectives they would like the team to be known for such as strong, kind, and resilient. Google the words, click images, and create a logo or a slogan for the team to remind them that the purpose and success of the team is always of a higher calling than going it alone.

5

STRESSING OVER BURNOUT

It begins with a spark of having no control.

People experience stress when they have to deliver results that are dependent on variables they can't control. This buildup of cumulative pressure to unsuccessfully direct the course of events necessary to complete a required task or goal, if gone unchecked, results in burnout.

The acceleration of chronic stress puts acute pressure on people's ability to cope in the moment, which sharply reduces their ability to manage it over time. It's like trying to quickly use a handheld vacuum before it's fully charged. There's a little bit of power surge at the beginning, but it keeps cutting out the more we try to make it work, until finally we resign and let the unit sit in the charger as long as the manual says it's supposed to.

Work has always been stressful in a positive and negative way to some degree. It's satisfying to tackle a problem, create a solution, and reap the reward of self-satisfaction by doing so. Almost everyone likes to check off a to-do item from their endless task list. When there's just enough stress to trigger the need to produce and it doesn't overtax the body and negatively impact the emotions, stress results in positive outcomes.

But if stress overtaxes the body and emotions, it can result in mental and physical illness. The World Health Organization describes burnout as "a syndrome conceptualized as resulting from chronic workplace stress that has not been successfully managed."

WHO'S FANNING THE BURNOUT FLAMES?

One of the long-standing organizational myths about burnout is that it stems from an employee's inability to manage stress and therefore is the responsibility of the employee to fix it. Traditionally, organizations have limited their role in stress management to that of a resource provider whose job is to offer training and third-party counseling programs to help employees deal with their issues.

With the recent surge of employees asking to be treated like human beings, companies are now looking more inward to determine whether their policies and programs are increasing or decreasing employees' stress levels. Gallup has said that if you put a good employee in a flawed system, the system wins every time. People leaders cannot do their part in setting a tone of mindful well-being for their direct reports if the company ties their hands with anti-well-being policies and procedures, whether formal or informal.

Excessive working hours, lack of flexible work sites, strict guidelines for taking time off, unclear expectations about availability and response windows (especially during supposed time off), and required attendance at excessive or non-pertinent meetings are just a few areas that companies need to examine through a lens of employee well-being.

For those employees working remotely, the daily pressure from the need to always be on, bombardment of emails, texts, instant messages, voice mails, conference calls, deadlines, ongoing interruptions, and now Zoom fatigue leaves few brain cells for the ability to accomplish any work with meaningful value. The overbuild of communication and collaboration tools and processes designed with the onset of working virtually has only contributed to burnout's intensity.

Employees continually confess they strive to get real work done while sitting in front of a live meeting screen and are multitasking on at least two to three activities simultaneously (hence the increase of dual monitor sales?).

DEATH BY BUSYNESS

How many times when you are asked to answer the question, "How's work going?" your response is always something like, "Busy" or "Slammed," or maybe "Crazy busy," or the triple dog doozey, "Totally insane busy!"

What gives with this culture of busyness we all have seemed to adopt? Does being busy suggest that we're in high demand? Or have a higher status? Or is it an unintended indicator of "help me" due to poor time management skills, inability to say no, or "I'm being held hostage by an oppressive boss"?

In any case such responses speak of a culture that says fanning burnout flames is accepted here. Being busy can definitely become a major culprit in adding a lot of unwanted weight to someone's Requirements side of their 3-R scale. There's a big difference between being busy and being productive. If you are hearing any level of busy as a candid reply when asking an employee, "How's it going?" it's worth exploring why.

Sometimes the pressure of needing to be perceived as busy can indicate a lack of trust with the leader, the organization, or both. This is often seen in cultures that manage an employee's performance by hours, volume, or degree of visibility instead of outcomes or results. Many remote workers are suffering from accelerated degrees of burnout because no one can see how hard they are working because they aren't seen coming in early, working through lunch, being the last to leave, or even coming in on a Saturday afternoon and running into a senior executive in the elevator.

All the previous visible indicators of busyness have been removed to the point remote workers are struggling to re-create them by always needing to be "on" at home. Maybe an alternative reply to the question, "How's work going?" that can get us away from just being busy would be to briefly describe your latest project, or problem you recently solved. Or just say "productive" or "engaging."

Anything but "busy"—it's not a status symbol.

PEOPLE DO WHAT THEIR LEADER DOES

What leaders say and how they behave has been proven to have a direct effect on their employees' stress and anxiety levels and hugely influences their team's physical and emotional well-being. The higher a leader's position in the organization, the more intense their impact both positively and negatively. Leaders who proudly display their badge of busyness drive a culture that paves the road to burnout.

Here are three tips to help you be the leader with the fire extinguisher instead of another match igniting more burnout flames:

- **Be mindful of how you're coming across when engaging the team members.** Your word choices, tone of voice, facial expressions, body language, and gestures are all powerful vehicles delivering your real message despite what you're saying. Your employees pick it all up, even an inborn sigh. If the team is sensing your stress, negativity, anxiety, or bad mood, because of your busyness, they will take on what they are observing. If you start wringing your hands in concern that the sky is falling, they will run for cover.

- **Avoid ambiguity and confusion.** Don't let being busy fuel more chaos and distract you from creating a sense of order and calm. There's enough busyness swirling around on its own right now. Senior leaders and business owners are creating and re-creating back-to-work plans by the minute. Vaccine mandates continue to inject clear-cut chaos into the workplace. Will I be fired if I don't? Will I keep my job if I do? The most important message here is to focus on what you can control right now and do it with the utmost clarity. Avoid wreaking havoc with people's calendars by making multiple schedule changes, last-minute cancellations, or missing a regularly scheduled 1:1. Send out a well-planned meeting agenda, have a timekeeper ensure the meeting stays on track. Be predictable, even a little boring. Now is definitely not the time to display unpredictable and busy behavior to keep everyone guessing what you might do next.

- **Stay tuned to your people's emotions.** When people leaders are hyperfocused on being busy, it can be easy to miss what's going on with the people you're leading. Make it safe for them to share their feelings. No judging or defending, just try to listen. Here's where a little bit of that empathy can go a long way.

TOP PERFORMERS, THEY FRY HARDER

Top performers are not the most likely ones to admit aloud to their leader, "I'm fried," but it doesn't mean they're not feeling that way. It may be somewhat surprising to learn that top performers are the most vulnerable to burnout. Their relentless focus on exceeding goals and successfully completing tasks makes them ripe for chronic stress that can quickly get out of control. They work extremely hard, mediocre is never acceptable, and they are in constant pursuit of excellence.

Top performers don't typically base their performance on extrinsic factors for motivation as much as they do intrinsic ones. They strive to surpass personal bests and end up competing with themselves. This intense drive of achievement energy can negatively end up displacing the internal support mechanism of self-care needed for recovery when outcomes and situations don't go their way. Their answer is to simply keep trying harder resulting in more frying harder instead.

Fear of failure prevents them from stopping long enough to meditate and rethink a new strategy, let alone take valuable time for a mindset of wellness and recovery. They tend to take care of work first and themselves as a distant second and can unintentionally become targets of abuse. Top performers are called top performers because they can always be depended on to make it happen. Even without optimal equipment, resources, or effective leadership, they still deliver and are too many times "rewarded" by being put on the next most critical project where the stakes are even higher and the stress even more intense.

Because top performers take and run with the big stuff, their leader can sometimes unconsciously depend on them for help with all the little stuff too. Too many casual requests like, "Hey, when you get a quick sec, would you mind doing, taking, creating, going, reviewing—? I know it will take *you* all of two minutes. If I give it to somebody else, it will take two weeks." Famous last words.

When managers make it a habit to ask top performers for help with even small tasks unrelated to their job's goals and objectives or to take up the slack for a nonperforming coworker, it's a recipe for burnout. Beware of layering unnecessary weight to their Requirements by seeking their help on administrative tasks or the management of low performers. Because top performers don't typically push back or complain, the leader is usually the one most surprised with their pronouncement of "I quit."

DO YOU KNOW WHERE YOUR TOP PERFORMER IS?

Top performers detest being micromanaged, and skilled people leaders fully get that, so once they trust their best employees' proven capabilities, they mistakenly tend to take a hands-off approach under the guise of granting them total autonomy. Too much autonomy is not advisable if their top performer also happens to be a human being.

Studies have shown that when employees are given the freedom associated with autonomy, it positively influences motivation and performance. Employees who feel they have the freedom to make choices in the workplace about how to do their job are happier and more productive. However, there is a risk of providing too much autonomy.

In a highly flexible and indirectly controlled work environment, too much job freedom may bring uncertainty and ambiguity, which will have the opposite effect and produce more stress. It has also been proven that too much job autonomy can reduce employee happiness and will aggravate job burnout by creating a potential for unethical behavior.

From a human aspect, excessive autonomy can turn into abandonment and will backfire when it results in the employee falling off their leader's radar. Top performers are people, too, and they don't run on autopilot. As human beings first and top performers second, they still have basic needs for personalized recognition, attention, self-esteem, belonging, respect, and being valued, to name a few. While the occasional "good job" or gratuitous reference to "rock star" is nice, it is a far cry from meaningful and ongoing feedback that drives personalized growth and development.

Spend as much time with them or more in 1:1 meetings. Routinely check in on their welfare and provide meaningful experiences and training opportunities that will promote their personal growth.

UNLIMITED TIME OFF IS NOT A BURNOUT STRATEGY

As a way to attract top-performing employees and prevent potential burnout, some organizations offer unlimited time off leaving it up to each employee to determine when they need time away from work for whatever reason and trust them to actually take it. The problem with that approach is top performers don't take time off because, well, they are too busy top performing. It's mostly the nonperformers who will take every minute possible to get away from work, sometimes even while on the job.

Top performers may be more compelled to take time away if it can't be accrued or cashed out. Many salaried employees who earn weeks of time off at the beginning of the year, end up not taking all their allotted time and lose what is left over. Some organizations provide the option to cash it out or apply the unused time toward an earlier retirement date. Unlimited paid time off isn't doing what it should as a solution to help reduce burnout.

One important aspect of a company's burnout prevention strategy is to promote a culture where time away is supported and encouraged especially for top performers. As a people leader, hold them accountable for actively owning ways to care for their own mental well-being, like taking time off and acknowledging them for doing so.

What we do know is that time away is a critical well-being factor of the job, and top performers don't come by it naturally. If needed, think about shifting to an RTO (required time off) policy where everyone in the organization is required to take time off as a proactive strategy on their part to prevent burnout.

WARNING LIGHTS

The first step to empowering people leaders with the ability to help their team manage stress and avoid burnout is to recognize the early warning signs. While each individual is different in their ability to tolerate stress and will react uniquely as they try to work through it, there are a number of universal warning signs to be aware of. Know your people and watch for extreme changes in their normal behaviors. If an extraverted, enthusiastic, and talkative employee has suddenly become sullen, introverted, and withdrawn, take note.

Here are few of the most common symptoms of potential burnout signs and ways to help:

- **Expressing feelings of tiredness or exhaustion:** Listen for complaints of not being able to sleep well or trouble with memory, recall, or fatigue. Do they have a voice in their schedules? Are they constantly working the third or night shift? Can a work shift or schedule adjustment be made? Are the shifts too long? Does the office setting provide direct sunlight? Can you ensure they get outside during the day? Is there a rest/power nap area? Frequent breaks?

- **Increased illnesses:** This situation can be a gray area and needs to be treated in a supportive way. Make sure your perception of missed workdays is validated with the data. Do you see any patterns? Is this change in attendance abrupt or historical? Ask what's going on in an empathetic way. Maybe there's a life change or the onset of unplanned circumstances at home. Listen and be supportive. Gently discipline and hold them accountable if you suspect insubordination.

- **Increased sensitivity to feedback or irritability:** Watch for overreactions, defensiveness, blaming, and a shutting down when given constructive feedback. Their nerves are on edge, and there is no bandwidth for a rational discussion. Kindly point out the change in behavior you are observing and invite them to talk about it and ways you can be more supportive.

- **Depression:** This is a common outcome of prolonged burnout. If you see a once-confident employee withdrawing and feeling insecure or expressing inordinate anxiety in fear of letting something fall through the cracks or missing a deadline, it is likely they are struggling with depression. Research is showing that remote workers are more susceptible to depression due to feelings of isolation and the constant need to be on. Don't make a diagnosis of depression on your own; leave that to a qualified professional. Gently reach out with empathy and share your observations to see if they are willing to discuss what is going on. Can time and resources be increased to help them meet deadlines?

- **Decreased passion for their work:** Especially with top performers, watch for waning enthusiasm and less joy on the job. Have they become jaded or more cynical about their work? Are you hearing "it doesn't matter anymore" or more complaints about the way they are being treated by you or the organization? Hold an honest dialogue about their concerns, ask for specific examples of what has negatively impacted their satisfaction, and address the concerns if possible. Can employees be more included in decision-making on processes and programs that affect them directly?

REMOTELY BURNING OUT

In addition to those burnout signs experienced by on-site employees, remote workers are showing additional stressors of what is being referred to as remote work fatigue. Even though 55% of employees say they will not work for an employer who doesn't offer a remote option, where possible, it doesn't mean that everyone is wired to successfully work from home.

While many desire the flexibility of working remotely, the research confirms that it doesn't come without a cost in terms of stress and burnout. *Forbes* recently reported that 69% of remote employees are experiencing burnout symptoms, negatively impacting productivity and mental health. And 93% of HR leaders have recently expressed increasing concerns about the burnout and mental well-being issues impacting remote employees.

If you have remote workers on the team, it's critical to take the time to fully understand the impact working from home has on each of them and how it's affecting the balance of their 3-R scale. For some employees it's a wonderful benefit they will refuse to give up. The significant increase to their Respect weight with a cherished freedom of flexibility, feelings of autonomy, not to mention the ability to do a load of laundry during the team meeting is so important, they are willing to trade off Rewards to keep it.

For others just the opposite is the case. They aren't doing well in that environment and their Requirements weight is getting heavier by the day as a result. Check out the primary reasons for remote worker burnout to see if any of these seem familiar as you think about each of your remote workers:

- **Fear of missing out (FOMO):** People as human beings are wired for social connections. Maslow refers to that as the basic need for belonging, and we see it clearly being played out among those working from home. The concern is being left out on critical updates, political intel, and all the nuances that only in-the-moment, face-to-face communication can provide.

- **Feelings of loneliness:** Remote workers are more likely to experience loneliness which can be an emotional trigger to feeling isolated and disconnected due to a lack of in-person interaction with their coworkers.

- **Always needing to be on mentality:** To counteract the anxiety of out of sight, out of mind, many remote workers are reporting that they are working twice as hard, with a 30% increase in hours just to maintain the same presence online as they felt they had on-site.

- **Missing out on professional development opportunities:** A critical part of on-the-job learning especially during the onboarding period comes from unplanned and informal mentoring by interacting with leaders and other coworkers. The loss of the ability to casually connect or observe their informal interactions can hamper professional growth.

- **Inadequate working environment:** Be it intermittent Wi-Fi, inadequate collaboration tools, lack of designated office space, continual homelife distractions, or bad ergonomics, the brain can only take so much before it implodes from unending interruptions, and mental acuity suffers.

- **Lack of discipline and accountability:** On the surface the freedom to work in pajamas (at least from the waist down) and donning a ball cap to fast-fix bed head may sound liberating, but the psychology behind it proves otherwise. Initiative tends to give way to apathy followed by a lack of mental keenness if a remote worker doesn't have the ability to compartmentalize work time from personal time. The discipline to be willing to look the part, act the part, and do the part during work hours is essential for establishing healthy mental boundaries.

TAKE FIVE

1. People leaders are subjected to an additional level of stress caring for their own mental welfare while trying to help employees work through their increasing stress levels.

2. Top performers are more vulnerable to burnout. Keep them on your radar, pay attention to their needs, don't abuse them with lower-level tasks and excessive lists of extra to-dos. Make sure they take regular time off.

3. While each individual is different in their ability to tolerate stress and will react uniquely as they try to work through it, there are a number of universal warning signs to be aware of. Know your people and watch for extreme changes in their normal behaviors.

4. For each employee working remotely, ask 3-R questions to clearly understand how the remote environment is impacting the balance of their Requirements, Rewards, and Respect weights. Remote burnout signs are in addition to on-site work stressors.

5. Use an empathetic approach when talking about burnout. Even switching up the infrequent and casual encounter of, "How's it going?" to "Tell me how you're feeling," "How are your expectations lining up with the reality you're experiencing?" "What are you loving? What is getting in your way?" will go a long way in the early identification of burnout and more proactively open up opportunity to manage it.

SURVIVAL TACTIC #1
GETTING MORE COMFORTABLE WITH AMBIGUITY AS A WAY TO COUNTERACT STRESS

One of the primary drivers of burnout and stress among leaders is living under the constant pressure of having to make decisions without always having 100% of the facts. The more you can get comfortable in working through ambiguity, and acting upon what you do know, the more resilience you can build from stressful indecision. Complete the assessment and refer to the following guide on improving your ability to deal with uncertainty and ambiguity as needed.

Read each statement and score your response using the following scale.

(1)	(2)	(3)	(4)	(5)
Strongly agree	Agree	Neutral	Disagree	Strongly disagree

STATEMENT	SCORE 1-5
1. I don't like working on problems that lack a clear-cut solution or outcome.	
2. I prefer having all the data before making a decision.	
3. I have a strong need to finish everything I start.	
4. The best way to solve issues is to apply tried-and-true solutions.	
5. I can balance many activities that are up in the air and still focus on getting results.	

STATEMENT	SCORE 1-5
6. It's important to get the "why" and the history before taking any next steps.	
7. I prefer details and specific directions before acting.	
8. When under pressure, I am less efficient and productive.	
9. Changes mostly result in rework or additional time needed to complete my work.	
10. I can comfortably shift gears in the moment.	
11. It upsets me when there's a sudden shift in priorities and my work is affected.	
12. I am afraid to fail and proceed cautiously as a result.	
Total	

48–60   Excellent: Ability to deal with uncertainty and go with the flow

36–47   Good: Can satisfactorily deal with change and move forward

24–35   Fair: Somewhat able to deal with uncertainty but decision-making may be hampered

12–23   Low: Inability to deal with uncertainty, restrained by stress and anxiety

WAYS TO HELP DEAL WITH AMBIGUITY AND UNCERTAINTY

Acceptance: It is impossible to predict the future. Instead of telling yourself that you have to be 100% certain all the time, write down how you would make decisions and move forward if you could be 80% certain.

Make small changes: Train yourself by making small, low-risk decisions. If you normally reread an important email three times, send it after two reviews. Break up habitual behaviors. If you normally have the same thing for lunch or eat in the same place, try something new and go somewhere different. Make a point to do something every day that is out of your normal routine.

Stop the fearful thinking: Many people struggle with ambiguity because of the fear of the unknown. Write down your source of the fear. Is it what others will think if you make a mistake? Fear of failing? Fear of being reprimanded?

Focus on past success: Because life is always uncertain, you already have a track record of dealing with ambiguity. Focus on the positive ways you have dealt with uncertainty in the past and apply what you've learned to any issues you're facing now.

Control what you can: Concentrate on what you can control, even if it's simple tasks, like running errands, meal planning, exercising, choosing to take some time each day for an activity you enjoy.

SURVIVAL TACTIC #2
HELP REMOTE WORKERS DEAL WITH ISOLATION

Many remote workers are combating feelings of being disconnected from the team and the organization. Help your remote team members feel more included with routine activities that encourage social interaction. Check out a few of these ideas:

Colleague Interview:

1. Set up a team online meeting. Pose a question like: *What was your favorite childhood toy? Why? Do you still have it? Best vacation? Your hero? If you could live anywhere? Proudest moment? Favorite movie? Book? Hobby? Food?*

2. Put two to three people in a Breakout room and have them interview each other on the one question you posed.

3. Return as a group and have the "interviewer" share what they learned from their partner.

Virtual Watercooler: Send a standing weekly invite to the team to voluntarily join the Watercooler for impromptu chat with other coworkers. You may wish to add a fun "topic of the week" for them to discuss, such as best vacation spot or worst food you've ever tried.

Team Meeting Kickoff Questions: Open up each team meeting with a kickoff question, similar to the examples in the Colleague Interview. Allow one to two minutes per person for their reply.

This Is My Life: Each month, have team members post a photo of something that represented their life that month. Have a few team members share their photo at each team meeting that month.

Guess the Desk: Each team member posts a close-up photo of their desk/workspace. Have team members guess whose space it belongs to.

Scavenger Hunt: Send a list of items for each team member to round up at home. Have team members share one or two of the items that they found: examples include favorite coffee mug, pet selfie, view from your window, family photo, wall art, pillow, board game, snack food.

Donut for Slack: As a casual opportunity for remote workers to chat and interact with each other 1:1, Donut (an app on Slack) randomly pairs team members from a predetermined list and distributes an email notification on a scheduled interval. It's up to the team members to coordinate their chat break.

6

"I QUIT" SIGNS AHEAD

Most top performers don't just randomly roll out of bed one morning and say, "Hey, I know, I think I'll quit my job today." The inclination to leave begins long before the proclamation.

Employee dissatisfaction can start to brew from the first day on the job and at any point after. If most of your turnover occurs within the first few months after employees start, it may be a red flag for discrepancies regarding what's promised during the recruiting process and the reality of the employee's experience on the job.

The best strategy to head off an "I quit" moment is to avoid being surprised by it in the first place, and the best surprise prevention tactic is to consistently have regular 3-R conversations to stay in touch with how each employee is feeling about the balance of their Requirements, Rewards, and Respect. It's also helpful to recognize warning signs that may indicate an employee is thinking about leaving.

Top performers who display a change in their normal behavior should be carefully assessed for any of the following signs that may indicate a decision to leave is on the horizon. It's important to note that one or two of these signs on their own could be an indicator of burnout, which, if not checked, is a precursor to quitting. However, if they are demonstrating a number of these red flags, it's essential that the leader have that 3-R conversation immediately.

TOP PERFORMER "I QUIT" SIGNS TO WATCH

- **"I'd love to, but—":** If this is the response when approaching a top performer about taking on a long-term project, it may indicate a hesitancy to commit to staying with the organization past their planned (but not revealed) exit date. They will push back with an insistence that they are too busy focusing on their current work when in reality they are wrapping things up in preparation to leave.

- **Active participation level decreases:** Watch for a decline in engagement. Instead of responding and providing input at team meetings, you observe a more passive role and less enthusiasm to get involved in the discussions. Top performers can be quite skilled in showing up to work without being present.

- **Decline in productive behavior:** Is your normally punctual top performer starting to show up late? Do you see responsibilities falling through the cracks causing your always dependable person to be less reliable? These behaviors can be indicators of distractions and focus on other activities outside of their work.

- **"Sorry, can't this time":** Watch for a decline in initiative. Top performers usually go out of their way to please their leader by volunteering to go beyond what is expected of them. An enthusiastic willingness to stay late, clean up without being asked, and take on extra work that has waned into apologies for not being able to can be an indicator that they are on the way out.

- **Increase in covert behavior:** You previously enjoyed an open and transparent relationship with your top performer and now there is a decline in their availability to want to connect, a delayed response to messages, and an overall decreased desire to communicate. If on-site, perhaps you've observed them blocking their computer screen, hitting a quick delete button, or covering up paperwork that may indicate a search is in process.

- **Gain of a surprise degree or certification:** Top performers are usually in pursuit of advancement and higher opportunities. If you are surprised that a top performer has been working on attaining a new degree, license, or certification, it can indicate a desire to become more attractive and marketable for new opportunities.

As previously noted, any one or two of these "I quit" warning signs may not necessarily result in a top performer's desire to leave the business; however, certain risky conditions may warrant more close examination if you see a warning sign within any of the following circumstances creating a higher risk scenario.

RISKY CONDITIONS

- **A change in the culture:** The culture of a team and of the organization as a whole is foundational to the well-being of employees and one of the primary drivers in their decision to leave or stay. Anytime there is a change in the culture due to a merger, acquisition, expansion, layoffs, or new senior leadership, the potential for employees leaving can become more intensified.

- **Passed over:** If a top performer felt they were a shoo-in for a promotion or key project assignment that did not happen, the setback can be enough to prompt their desire to look elsewhere. Promised raises that are not fulfilled when expected may also result in the same drive to move on.

- **Stagnation:** Top performers tend to become quickly bored when they are no longer challenged. If they have been in the same role for too long and feel no sense of moving within the organization to gain new skills and experiences, they will look elsewhere for the next, bigger opportunity.

- **Negative interactions with others:** Whenever people mix, the potential for conflict will inevitably happen. Pay close attention to how your team members are interacting with each other. Watch the online meetings for tone, eye rolling, or any subtle smirks of exasperation you see exchanged. Sometimes the pushback to work with another colleague can be more obvious in the refusal to take on collaborative projects together. It must be addressed, or the negativity will continue to spread, infecting the entire team.

- **Change in team leader:** Because of the direct impact a top performer's leader has on their basic needs such as safety, belonging, and fulfillment, this is the most critical condition to assess. If their previous leader was toxic, the change will likely be a welcomed sigh of relief. Losing a leader who was ideal sets up the potential for additional risks. Either way, pay close attention if any of the "I quit" signs begin to emerge in this situation.

- **Personal circumstances:** Life itself can often be the single driver behind an employee's decision to leave, be it family challenges, health issues, or something else. All the more important to get to know each of your people as individuals and, if possible, proactively provide a solution or the support to work through it and enable them to stay.

BEST NOT TO FOLLOW YOUR GUT ON THIS ONE

How many times have you been told to just go with your gut when making decisions? That may be a consideration when it is impossible to acquire all the information necessary to make an informed one. But if you are a people leader working directly with your team members, a lack of available information isn't so much the case.

One of the most ineffective approaches a people leader can use in a potential turnover scenario is to independently act on a hunch and miss key factors in the equation, or to make assumptions and execute an incorrect approach thus making the situation worse. For example, businesses can tend to overgeneralize employees' needs especially when it comes to money. Yes, it's a driver of retention in some cases but not always so, and the unfortunate result is to see businesses spend hundreds of thousands of dollars in blanket increases with no major impact on improving retention.

The most effective way to engage and influence people in the workplace is to get to know each one of them as an individual person. When it comes to understanding how to retain people, the average employee doesn't exist nor is there such a thing as a one-size-fits-all program where people are concerned. Everybody is an amalgamation of different experiences and influences that have shaped them into the people they are at this moment. And like an iceberg, that shape can morph and change with the mere exposure to everyday life.

Stay in tune, watch for changes in your top performers' demeanor. Be ready as appropriate to address their needs. On any given day, someone may have just placed an aging parent into eldercare, committed a child to rehab, finalized a divorce, adopted a child, received unwelcomed health news—any of these types of experiences may directly impact your employees' inclination to leave or stay and you'll want to be able to proactively address it beforehand.

BETTER LATE THAN TOO LATE FOR A 3-R CONVERSATION

If you are reading this and perhaps thinking something like, "Sure wish I knew then what I'm learning now," take heart, it may not be too late. While not as ideal as holding preventive 3-R conversations to keep close tabs on how each employee is feeling about the balance of the job Requirements, with the Rewards and Respect they are getting in return, taking that approach now may at least help to clarify the pain points and more easily determine if the situation is salvageable.

Don't begin a 3-R conversation by pointing out any of the "I quit" warning signs you may have seen. If a top performer is already set on working their exit plan, your proclaimed observations at this point will likely be met with denial or a claim of misinterpretation on your part.

Instead, lead an explanation of what the 3-Rs represent and open the discussion with something like this: *Because we're all challenged with running in a million directions right now and trying to maintain some sort of mental well-being, I would like to check in on how you are feeling about your workload in general and if it's in balance with what you're getting in return right now. What part of the job Requirements are adding extra pressure? Are the Rewards valuable in the way you would personally define a Reward? What changes could be explored as a result? What about Respect? To what degree do you feel valued, appreciated, and cared for? What can I do better as result?*

In retrospect you can probably see how much more valuable this conversation would have been from the start with the need to only make small tweaks along the way, as opposed to an emergency intervention in the attempt to salvage a mind already made up. But at least it's worth a try sooner than later to see if the root of the issues can be uncovered and addressed.

QUIT HAPPENS, PREPARE A PEOPLE PLAN

No matter our attempts, there are situations where we can't make people stay and resignations are going to happen. We can only aim to reduce the number of top talent resignations by deploying every tool possible. The exact reason someone leaves their job may not be within your control, but in the majority of those cases where it is, prevention is always better than the cure.

You may encounter that perpetually dissatisfied employee whose life career is the pursuit of their own unhappiness. But the majority of the time a disengaged employee is experiencing a severe tilt in the balance of their 3-R scale, and it's something their people leader can address by treating people as individual human beings and recognizing their unique motivators and needs.

Despite our best efforts when the inevitable comes and leaving is the only outcome, have a backup plan to mitigate the impact. Consider these seven points to help you and your team absorb the impact of an unpreventable resignation:

1. Make a list of the key roles on your team.

2. Identify the most critical skills needed for each of the key roles.

3. Make a list of each of the people on your team.

4. Identify the strengths and skill sets of each person.

5. Map the team's skill sets to each of the roles.

6. Note where there may be skill gaps as well as duplications for all positions.

7. Create a plan to address the gaps. Can employees be cross-trained for certain areas? Can some tasks be centralized to free up resources for other needs?

HELLO, REMEMBER ME?

In the frantic flurry of addressing turnover issues, hiring more staff, and simply trying to keep the doors open in some cases, a group that can easily get pushed to the side or lost in the shuffle are the ones who are still there—your work warriors who show up day in and day out and not only carry out their job duties but are also silently shouldering the work of those who left. Could there be a more critical time to make sure you keep them? It's not like people leaders have an overabundance of bandwidth these days, and it can be easy to overlook what appears to be running well.

Your existing people need you more than ever, and it's time to shower each one with the appreciation and recognition they deserve. Be hyperaware of your impact on them and the additional workloads they may be carrying right now. You're apparently effective either consciously or unconsciously in making sure your remaining employees' 3-R scales have remained in balance.

Let's look at five themes emerging among those leaders who are ensuring the 3-R scales stay in balance:

1. **Keep talking and personally connecting.** Now is not the time to let up on having regular 3-R conversations about the weight of their Requirements, Rewards, and Respect the employees are experiencing. They're taking on extra workloads and you want to ensure the Rewards and Respect are keeping up.

2. **Show an abundance of appreciation.** There can't be too much gratitude expressed to this group right now. Make it a point to provide positive feedback to someone every day. Make it more than just a complimentary thank-you or "keep up the great work." Call out something specific they did, name the positive behaviors you observed, and say how their action helped the entire team as a result. Compliments are nice, but positive feedback delivered in that way is extremely powerful.

3. **Empower team members to show gratitude to each other.** Implement a thank-you board or post where coworkers can acknowledge how another team member helped and supported them. Provide nominal gift cards that could be included in the gesture.

4. **Include the team in designing flexible return-to-work options.** If remote or hybrid working is an alternative, include

the team's input on ways to make it work effectively. One-size-fits-all policies and mandates about how conditions will be for returning to work is potentially a message that the employees' needs and concerns are not important in this key decision-making process.

5. **Keep rallying around the team's mission and purpose.** Focus on the higher calling of why the team is working so hard. People are craving to feel valued and have a sense they belong to something bigger than their day-to-day tasks. Keep fostering their shared sense of purpose and how each one is also individually making a difference.

If you're in the group that is not seeing significant turnover, don't assume that circumstances can't shift. Stay vigilant and care for each of your people as individuals. There are a lot of people in the workplace right now—many of them are top performers who are trying to handle their burnout by putting on a positive game face every morning to mask their own struggles. Model the care that you want to see the team give to each other and make it okay to ask for help by doing that yourself.

TAKE FIVE

1. Most top performers don't randomly quit. The inclination to leave begins long before the proclamation.

2. Watch for "I quit" signs such as hesitancy to take on long-term projects, decreased participation, decline in productivity, decline in taking initiative, covert behavior, and completion of a surprise degree or certification.

3. Watch for risky conditions that may foster reasons for leaving such as a change in culture, passed over for an expected promotion, stagnation in role, new team leader, and personal circumstances.

4. Create a people backup plan in the event of an unplanned loss of an existing employee. Note your strengths and vulnerabilities and any ways to mitigate the impact.

5. It's as important to pay close attention and care for the employees who are staying as well as for the ones you think may be leaving.

SURVIVAL TACTIC #1
AT-RISK EMPLOYEE ASSESSMENT

Most employees don't decide to randomly quit on the spot. There are signs to watch for. Review the following "I quit" signs and note any employees that may be at risk. Hold a 3-R conversation as soon as possible to learn if the Requirements, Rewards, or Respect may be out of balance.

"I QUIT" SIGN	TEAM MEMBERS AT RISK
"I'd love to, but—" If this is the response when approaching a top performer about taking on a long-term project, it may indicate a hesitancy to commit to staying with the organization past their planned exit date.	
Active participation level decreases Watch for a decline in engagement. Instead of responding and providing input at team meetings, you observe a more passive role and less enthusiasm to get involved in the discussions. Top performers can be quite skilled in showing up to work without being present.	
Decline in productive behavior Is your normally punctual top performer starting to show up late? Do you see responsibilities falling through the cracks causing your always dependable person to be less reliable? These behaviors can be indicators of distractions and focus on other activities outside of their work.	

"I QUIT" SIGN	TEAM MEMBERS AT RISK
"Sorry, can't this time" Watch for a decline in initiative. Top performers usually go out of their way to please their leader by volunteering to go beyond what is expected of them. An enthusiastic willingness to stay late, clean up without being asked, and take on extra work that has waned into apologies for not being able to can be an indicator that they are on the way out.	
Increase in covert behavior There is a decline in their availability to want to connect, a delayed response to messages, and an overall decreased desire to communicate. If on-site, perhaps you've observed them blocking their computer screen, hitting an emergency delete button, or covering up paperwork that may indicate a search is in process.	
Gain of a surprise degree or certification Top performers are usually in pursuit of advancement and higher opportunities. If you are surprised that a top performer has been working on attaining a new degree, license, or certification, it can indicate a desire to become more attractive and marketable for new opportunities.	

SURVIVAL TACTIC #2
PREPARE A PEOPLE PLAN

The best strategy for managing the vacancies among your team is to proactively prepare ways you can mitigate the loss. Start by mapping out the roles, skills, and current people in the positions.

POSITION NAME	CRITICAL SKILLS NEEDED

TEAM MEMBER	STRENGTHS	WEAKNESSES

PEOPLE PLAN REVIEW QUESTIONS

- Review each of the roles on your team and note the critical skills.

- Review the strengths among your team members. How do these strengths map to the skills you need for each role?

- Is there an overabundance of team skills in a certain area?

- Are there any critical skills needed that the team is missing?

- How can those critical skill gaps be addressed?

- Where can team members be cross-trained to cover these areas?

- Can any tasks be centralized to free up team members to gain these critical skills?

- If the person currently in any role decided to leave, what is the backup plan to cover the tasks?

PART III

WILL I STAY OR WILL I GO? (YES, BUT IT DEPENDS)

Whether an employee chooses to stay or leave an organization comes down to a simple balancing act. If the Requirements being asked of them balance with the Rewards and Respect they are getting in return, they will most likely stay. An employee may choose to stay in some situations as long as the Rewards outweigh the Requirements despite the Respect being dismally low, or when the Respect outweighs the Requirements even though the Rewards are lower than desired. In either case the employee is a flight risk. This section will explain in detail how the 3-R scale works and what people leaders can do to create and maintain its optimal balance.

7

THE GREAT BALANCING ACT: INTRODUCING THE 3-R SCALE

Turnover is a personal issue and must be treated as such,
by first understanding how each unique employee defines
Requirements, Rewards, and Respect.

Do you remember playing with a plastic toy scale as a kid? The one that came with many brightly colored pieces in various shapes and weights, and the goal was to hang the correct pieces on the opposite sides of the scale so it would balance. The challenge was in figuring out which piece or combination of pieces would counterbalance the others to achieve that perfectly balanced state.

This simple metaphor of a toy scale describes the mental process an employee uses to decide whether they will leave or stay with their employer. It's called the 3-R scale, named for the three pieces used to achieve the ideal balance in their job. They will ponder the Requirements needed to succeed at the job, the Rewards received in return for doing the job, and the degree of perceived Respect they are feeling from their leader and the organization while on the job.

The balancing act of a 3-R scale begins with the employee placing the Requirements piece on one side of the scale. Requirements are any of the demands they must fulfill to be successful at the job. They may be direct or indirect.

Direct Requirements occur while actually doing the job, like scheduled to work a Sunday shift, sitting down all day, or stuffed into a cramped space with a sunflower-seed-spitting coworker. Indirect Requirements happen as a secondary outcome from accepting the job and tend to impact the employee's personal life such as the need to arrange for childcare, commuting to the office during peak traffic, or missing a child's soccer game due to meeting conflicts.

On the opposite side of the scale, the employee will next place the Rewards and the Respect pieces and then take a step back to assess the scale's balance. If the combined Rewards and Respect weights balance the weight of the Requirements, the employee will feel a sense of contentment, be satisfied in their role, and, most importantly, will choose to stay in it as a result.

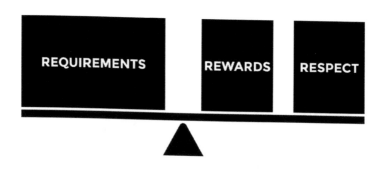

A balanced 3-R scale.

If, however, the Requirements outweigh the Rewards and Respect, the employee will feel the opposite, and the imbalance will likely result in their leaving unless an adjustment is made to any of the three weights to bring the scale into balance.

So there you have it. Employee retention is as simple as balancing a child's toy. Ha! One can only wish. Where it gets interesting for people leaders striving to keep an employee's 3-R scale in balance especially for top performers is the hidden weight differentials each individual will assign to any of the pieces. For example, let's use one of the most common rewards of money to see how that principle works.

MONEY AND MOTIVATION MAKE STRANGE BEDFELLOWS

True or false: Money is a powerful motivator.
Answer: It depends on who you're motivating.

In the 1970s Edward Deci, a professor of psychology at the University of Rochester, ran an experiment showing how incentivizing students with money to solve puzzles actually made them less interested in working on them after being paid. Meanwhile, another group of students **who hadn't been offered money** worked on the puzzles longer and with more interest. Deci's findings, gleaned from many similar studies he conducted, were that money does not always mean better performance. His work uncovered the powerful and significant difference between **extrinsic motivation** from outside sources and **intrinsic motivation** from within oneself.

Money is definitely a driver that will get people working. A lack of fair and equitable starting pay continues to make headlines behind the top reasons employees are leaving their jobs. It's easy for someone with a lot of money to say that money isn't everything. While research confirms that more money does not positively correlate to more happiness, the absence of it for fundamental basics like food, water, and transportation—resources most of us take for granted—can be a powerful factor that heavily impacts behavior. Once basic needs are met, the value of money becomes subjective. However, additional money will not necessarily motivate people to work harder or to stay with their employer.

ALL WEIGHTS ARE NOT CREATED EQUAL

A critical piece to understanding how employees will balance their 3-R scale must first start with knowing how each person defines Requirements, Rewards, and Respect within a job setting. Making any assumptions without knowing the facts can result in complete miscalculations of what matters most to the individuals we wish to motivate. A specific part of an employee's Requirements weight can be heavy or light depending on how much weight the person assigns to it.

While a one-hour commute in peak traffic may be a major source of Requirements stress for some, for others it may not be a Requirements burden at all, but a welcomed time to listen to music, an entire podcast, or just to think and unwind before taking on additional challenges at home. Each Requirement by itself is neutral; it's the person's reaction to the Requirement and the personalized amount of weight they assign to it that matters.

The same consideration is also true for how an employee will define the Reward and Respect weights. Why this point is so critical to grasp from the beginning is that, as human beings, people leaders can fall prey to projecting their own assessment of what constitutes a Requirement, Reward, or action of Respect and assume their people would likewise. Because the leader may not particularly welcome an aspect of the job doesn't always mean someone else wouldn't. We can't be sure until we engage in the conversations with each individual to find out.

The opposite is true too. What a leader might deem as a Reward, others may not attach the same value to. Taking the team out for some Friday afternoon fun with drinks and ax throwing may not be welcomed by all. As we know, one person's trash is another person's treasure and so is the case with one employee's Requirements being another employee's Reward.

Neither the organization nor the leader can assume how much weight each person will assign to each of their 3-Rs—only the individual employee can do that. As a result, companies fall into an assumption trap and try to implement one-size-fits-all retention programs and policies with little impact to turnover as a result. Turnover is a personal issue and is treated by first understanding how each unique employee defines Requirements, Rewards, and Respect.

TAKE FIVE

1. In deciding to leave or stay, employees will ponder the Requirements needed to succeed at the job, the Rewards received in return for doing the job and the degree of perceived Respect they are feeling from their leader and the organization while on the job.

2. Direct Requirements occur while actually doing the job. Indirect Requirements happen as a secondary outcome from accepting the job and tend to impact the employee's personal life.

3. More money does not positively correlate to more happiness. However, the absence of money to access fundamental basics like food, water, and transportation—resources most of us take for granted—can be a powerful factor that heavily impacts behavior.

4. A critical piece to understanding how employees will balance their 3-R scale must first start with knowing how each person defines Requirements, Rewards, and Respect within a job setting.

5. Neither the organization nor the leader can assume how much weight each person will assign to each of their 3-Rs; only the individual employee can do that.

SURVIVAL TACTIC
SAME ROLE, TWO PERSPECTIVES EXERCISE

Employees doing the same job will likely have different perspectives on its pluses and minuses, which is important to know when balancing a 3-R scale. Consider two team members who have the same general responsibilities. List the job tasks, add each team member's name, and note how you think each one would rate that task, as a plus or a minus part of their job. Have them independently confirm your guesses.

JOB TASK	TEAM MEMBER		TEAM MEMBER	
	+	-	+	-

8

REQUIREMENTS: WHAT WILL THIS JOB NEED ME TO DO?

*The most detrimental Requirement an organization can expect
an employee to meet is to tolerate a culture or leader who
doesn't make them feel emotionally and mentally safe.*

Depending on an employee's initial level of excitement in landing the position, that blissful honeymoon period where everything is new and hopeful and where positive anticipation is at its peak is initially enticing and may distract the new hire from seeing many of the real Requirements yet to surface. Therefore, the total weight of the direct and indirect Requirements an employee will assign to their job takes some time to settle.

It's somewhat like a kid wanting a new puppy. Every possible need for future Fido's care will be happily doable and committed to up front. It isn't until the reality of routine daily feedings, yard cleanup, walks, potty training, and behavior coaching sets in that the realization of anticipating Fido was a lot more fun than the real Fido turned out to be.

Once the full picture of the job begins to unfold, the true weight of the Requirements falls into position on the 3-R scale. Some Requirements, usually the direct ones, are easily identifiable from the beginning as spelled out in the job posting. It's the indirect Requirements that are not as detectable until time on the job has passed. For example, when the recruiter says the hours are 9 a.m. to 5 p.m. but after two months the reality of 5 p.m. is more like 6 p.m. and with no compensating Rewards, the Requirements weight just got a lot heavier.

The following chart provides examples of the types of direct Requirements that may be clear at the start and indirect Requirements that may begin to surface over time. Remember, the actual weight assigned to any of them will be up to the individual employee to determine and for their people leader to find out.

DIRECT AND INDIRECT REQUIREMENTS LIST	
DIRECT	**INDIRECT**
• Strenuous physical activities	• Commute time/costs
• Exposure to physical safety hazards	• Commute options: auto/train/bus/ferry
• Standing/sitting all day	• Sleep/exercise schedule
• Inside/outside environment	• Meal/lunch prep
• In front of a computer all day	• Nutrition/physical care
• Vaccinations/masks/tests	• Purchase of clothing, equipment
• Unavailability of leader	• Personal grooming
• Number of direct reports	• Availability for errands/home management
• On-site only/remote only	• Work time crossing over into personal time
• Extensive travel/after-hours events	
• Fast-/slow-paced culture	• Inability to attend family events
• Lack of organizational strategy	• Decreased social activities
• Unfulfilling work	• Isolation issues/working remotely
• Lack of diversity/inclusion	• Childcare needs
• Toxic culture/mistrust	• Parenting concerns
• Lack of communication	• Pet care needs
• Unclear goals/expectations	• Eldercare needs
• Toxic boss	• Inability to pursue sports/hobbies
• Psychological safety	• Level of mental energy available off work
• Adapting to constant change	
• Work start/stop times	• Personal/family burnout
• Expectations of response time	• Reassessment of work as validation
• Lack of planning	• Reassessment of life goals
	• Lack of higher purpose/boredom
	• Lack of control in general

THE UNFORGIVABLE REQUIREMENT: LACK OF PSYCHOLOGICAL SAFETY

It's almost impossible to read anything about employee retention today that doesn't mention lack of mental well-being or psychological safety as a primary driver behind people leaving their jobs; therefore, it bears special treatment when talking about the Requirements of doing the job.

The most detrimental Requirement an organization can expect an employee to meet is to tolerate a culture or leader that doesn't make them feel emotionally and mentally safe. In those cases, the employees' Requirements weight will become so heavy that almost any combination of Rewards and Respect won't be enough to counterbalance it. The Great Resignation proved it. The primary reason employees cited for leaving their job was that "the emotional and mental toxicity was just not worth it."

What does it mean exactly to be psychologically safe and what should a people leader be doing to promote employees' mental well-being and safety?

Organizational development researchers in the 1960s first identified concerns for emotional and psychological safety as a critical factor among those employees reporting stress and anxiety. To feel emotionally or psychologically safe, employees must feel free to be themselves, have a voice, and know that there is a trusted outlet where they can speak up about issues of particular importance to them. They want the empowerment to take risks and admit mistakes without adverse repercussions.

Because the boundary lines between work life and personal life have become so blurred, employees expect an organization to embrace them holistically as individuals and not as cogs in an endless production wheel. Their expectation is not that the job will be free from stress but that there will be an established climate where stress can be processed and resources available as needed to deal with it.

In addition to the need for safety, the basic human need for belonging is also at play here. None of us wants to wake up with a stomach full of dread each morning as we contemplate the workday. People need to feel comfortable and welcomed to be themselves where they can feel like what they contribute to the business is valued and appreciated.

WHAT'S A PEOPLE LEADER TO DO?

Most people leaders don't start work every morning by wondering what they can do that day to create an unsafe psychological work environment for their employees. It's like weeds in a garden—no one purposely cultivates their growth; weeds just sort of crop up and take over due to a lack of attention. Like weeds, the lack of a psychologically safe environment can simply be an unconscious oversight. Some leaders just don't have the need to create a mentally safe environment on their radar or aren't convinced that perpetuating one has any direct impact on employee engagement and retention.

Sometimes a leader is misled by a team who can fool them into thinking everything is fine and productive when actually each individual is wearing their work mask of unspoken compliance behaviors necessary to survive. Other leaders may be fully aware of the need to create mental safety but don't know how to go about it and thus discredit its impact or hold the employee accountable for not being able to deal with what the leader deems is a personal issue for the employee to solve.

The first step toward creating a psychologically safe environment is to recognize the positive team behaviors people demonstrate when they do have a sense of belonging and mental safety. See how your team measures up to the following indicators of the presence of psychological safety:

- Feedback among the team flows naturally with many delivery channels. People freely ask for positive as well as constructive ideas on how they can continue to grow.

- Diversity of thought is welcomed and encouraged. Counterpoints are invited. People actively share opinions that differ from those of other team members and their leader.

- Leaders encourage critical thinking by asking for team feedback on the pros as well as the cons on projects, policies, and programs that will impact them.

- In project status or 1:1 meetings, employees easily share what's at risk and where they need help in addition to what's going well. They avoid blame in the desire to build trust.

- There's no covert, after-meeting chatter among cliques or alliances trying to decode what was really said and where they stand as a result.

- The leader is rarely surprised by a negative outcome. Information is power. Employees who feel psychologically safe easily come to their leader with what's going well and what isn't going so well. Those that don't, withhold it and the leader is the last to know.

Bottom line: one of the best employee retention practices that people leaders can start with right now is to ensure that the level of psychological safety on the team is where it needs to be and closely monitor the climate to make sure it stays that way. This is just as critical if not more so with remote employees.

HAVE A 3-R REQUIREMENTS CONVERSATION

It's never too early to have your employee weigh in about the Requirements needed to successfully do the job. Which of the direct and indirect ones are impacting them the most? How much weight are they assigning to each? A simple place to start would be to have a casual conversation around the roles and responsibilities of their job, call them the direct Requirements, and share the concept of balancing a scale. For example, you're talking with your new sales representative about a few of the direct Requirements of their job such as cold calling, product demonstrations, overnight travel, completing reports, and training new representatives.

Ask them to think about assigning a 1 to 5 weight factor to each Requirement with a 1 representing the lightest weight and a 5 representing the heaviest weight that aspect of the role has on their job satisfaction. The employee is not going to equally love doing every one of those activities and will likely rank them differently, somewhere between 1 and 5. In the coming chapters you will see just how valuable this information will be if there is a need to recalibrate their scale back into balance by either lightening the Requirements weight or increasing the Reward and Respect weights.

Next, explain the concept of indirect Requirements. These are the more personal impacts as a result of having taken the position such as needing childcare, time away from family, or missing an important event. Be careful in discussing the indirect Requirements so as not to appear prying into someone's personal life as a potential indicator of their ability to succeed at the job. Consider approaching the conversation with something like this: *I more than understand how work and personal life all tends to get blended together these days, and I want to be sure you keep a healthy balance of being able to do both well. Please keep me informed of any support you may need if you start to feel something is getting out of balance.*

That's about as close as you want to go. Do not have them weight the items on the potential indirect Requirements list. Asking a question like, "Is arranging for childcare a concern?" will quickly get you into HR trouble. If you have built a culture of psychological safety, employees will feel free to come to you and share any indirect Requirement concerns in time. The list offered in this chapter is just for you to get a sense of the types of impact. Once your employee willingly shares that information, you'll have more clarity on what may be needed to additionally balance their scale if needed.

TAKE FIVE

1. The total weight of the direct and indirect Requirements an employee will assign to their job takes some time to settle.

2. Some Requirements, usually the direct ones, are more easily identifiable from the beginning as spelled out in the job posting. It's the indirect Requirements that are not as identifiable until time on the job has passed.

3. Indirect Requirements are more personal in nature and can be discussed only when the employee willingly feels comfortable to share them.

4. The most detrimental Requirement an organization can expect an employee to meet is to tolerate a culture or leader that doesn't make them feel emotionally and mentally safe.

5. The first step toward creating a psychologically safe environment is to recognize the positive team behaviors people demonstrate when they do have a sense of belonging and mental safety.

SURVIVAL TACTIC
HAVE A 3-R REQUIREMENTS CONVERSATION

It's important to have your employees weigh in about the Requirements needed to successfully do the job and understand how the direct and indirect Requirements are impacting them. Start by holding a Requirements conversation with your top performers:

Begin the conversation: *I want us to stay connected on making sure the weight of your total tasks feels balanced for what you're receiving in return. It's important for me to understand which of the Requirements will impact you in both a positive and negative way. There are two types of Requirements: the direct tasks that need completing as part of the actual job [provide examples for their specific role] and the indirect Requirements that typically impact us in a more personal way as a result of the job, like commuting, setting up a home office, and the like. Here are some examples of direct and indirect Requirements: [share Sample Job Requirements]*

Let's look at your direct Requirements and assess their weight. List the ones impacting you in your current role and assign a weight from 1 to 5. A score of 1 is the least impactful or puts the least amount of stress on you, and a score of 5 would be the heaviest weight and most impact on you.

REQUIREMENTS ASSESSMENT

Team Member_____ Date_____

SAMPLE JOB REQUIREMENTS	
DIRECT	**INDIRECT**
• Strenuous physical activities • Exposure to physical safety hazards • Standing/sitting all day • Inside/outside environment • In front of a computer all day • Vaccinations/masks/tests • Unavailability of leader • Number of direct reports • On-site only/remote only • Extensive travel/after-hours events • Fast-/slow-paced culture • Lack of organizational strategy • Unfulfilling work • Lack of diversity/inclusion • Toxic culture/mistrust • Lack of communication • Unclear goals/expectations • Toxic boss • Psychological safety • Adapting to constant change • Work start/stop times • Expectations of response time • Lack of planning	• Commute time/costs • Commute options: auto/train/bus/ferry • Sleep/exercise schedule • Meal/lunch prep • Nutrition/physical care • Purchase of clothing, equipment • Personal grooming • Availability for errands/home management • Work time crossing over into personal time • Inability to attend family events • Decreased social activities • Isolation issues/working remotely • Childcare needs • Parenting concerns • Pet care needs • Eldercare needs • Inability to pursue sports/hobbies • Level of mental energy available off work • Personal/family burnout • Reassessment of work as validation • Reassessment of life goals • Lack of higher purpose/boredom • Lack of control in general

List the major direct and indirect Requirements of your job as of today. Rank the degree of weight each of these direct Requirements is adding to your 3-R scale.

(1) None   (2) Slight   (3) Neutral   (4) Substantial   (5) Major

DIRECT REQUIREMENTS	RATING 1-5
INDIRECT REQUIREMENTS (OPTIONAL) **AS YOU FEEL COMFORTABLE, FEEL FREE TO SHARE ANY INDIRECT REQUIREMENTS AND RANK.**	

9

REWARDS: WHAT AM I GETTING IN RETURN FOR DOING THIS JOB?

Meaningful Rewards can be anything—
from a token bag of candy to a significant cash award.

Once an employee places their initial Requirements weight on the 3-R scale, the next important piece they will consider is the weight of the Rewards they are getting in return. People work for various reasons: money, recognition, advancement, validation, financial security, fulfillment, or all of the above.

Competitive compensation carries more weight for top performers because of their ability to generate revenue for the business. They will expect more pay proportionally. The challenge, however, with increasing compensation as a universal attraction for entry-level positions is that the impact of its value is short term. Typically, a pay raise takes three to six months to blend into an employee's landscape and become a nonevent. Then the zing factor is gone. Employees next look to additional rewards such as benefit packages, 401(k)s, certifications, commissions, growth opportunities, and bonuses or time off as additional ways to balance the weight of the Requirements they must meet.

There are two primary types of Rewards: intrinsic and extrinsic. Intrinsic Rewards are driven by an individual's internal motivators, such as a sense of pleasure or accomplishment when achieving a personal best goal. Extrinsic Rewards are outside of the individual. They are tangible items offered by a leader or organization in return for successfully meeting the job Requirements. Tangible Rewards such as money become essential as motivators only if the lack of them exists.

Financial Rewards will always play a part in an employee's decision to leave or stay if they sense any inequities in fairness. It's interesting to note that since the pandemic many employees are putting more value on nonfinancial Rewards such as feeling appreciated for the work they do or finding a position that better serves their need for mental well-being and better fits their description of work-life balance.

A REWARD BY ANY OTHER NAME MAY NOT SMELL AS SWEET

As with Requirements, every employee will assign a different weight of value to any type of Reward. Paychecks, commissions, bonuses, stock options, equity, 401(k), stipends, paid time off, healthcare coverage, pet insurance, gym membership, day care, phone allowance, home office setup allowance, transportation reimbursement, expense account, company car, title, education reimbursement, professional coach, recognition awards, training opportunities, certifications, continuing education credits, student loan repayments, and special recognition events will all carry completely different values depending on the employee.

Because people leaders and organizations may wrongly assume what an employee values as a Reward, there are many misses when it comes to handing them out. Many employees would much rather have a $25 gift card to their favorite fast-food place than a $200 dinner out with their boss. Prior to the pandemic when working from home was not a regular part of life, some organizations decided to boldly proclaim a "work from home" day as a special reward on every other Friday.

Sounds fun, but for the parent with four kids who had to hole up in the bathroom to get the month-end report out on time, it was not a Reward. And truth be known, more than one high performer privately dreaded the nine-day trip to China as a hand-selected member of a top talent development opportunity. It's no wonder why so many companies score consistently low for reward and recognition categories on annual surveys. Meaningful Rewards are defined only by the person receiving them.

Even the way a Reward is presented can have the opposite effect of its intended purpose, as was the case of a top-performing project manager who was in absolute shock when called to take center stage in front of 300 coworkers at a company award ceremony. Once handed the plaque to roaring cheers from the audience, his desire to cut for the exit was thwarted with thunderous chants of "Speech! Speech!" at which point he expressed a timid, "Thank you, but it should go to the team," before a prompt exit.

The next day upon seeing his leader in the hallway, he thanked them again for the award but confessed he was a card-carrying introvert and mortified by the public fanfare, and while most appreciative of the gesture pleaded never to have that situation happen again, noting that a simple thank-you email would have more than sufficed. Leader thought, okay, lesson learned.

Imagine the untended consequences of that lesson learned when the same leader recognized a different employee with a special award the following month. This time instead of risking another public mortification response, the leader decided to send a heartfelt thank-you email instead. Much to the chagrin of the recipient, the email was a disappointment as this person loved limelight and applause, thus feeling wholly unappreciated as a result. Can't win? Only if you don't know your employees' recognition preferences.

REWARDS COME IN ALL SIZES

Meaningful Rewards that carry a lot of weight can be anything from a token bag of candy to a significant cash award. This was especially true for a young, new supervisor assigned to lead a seasoned team of tenured individuals in the cable industry. Sam, a team member who had been with the company for over twenty-five years, was particularly difficult to connect with and chose to remain distant and aloof from the team and from the new supervisor as much as possible. To try and rally team camaraderie, Maleep, the supervisor, staged a few social events, which Sam never attended.

One afternoon Maleep happened to catch Sam make a rare appearance in the breakroom to purchase a bag of Skittles. They shared no more than a quick hello and "Have a nice evening." About a month later Maleep received a copy of a glowing review a customer had sent to the company about Sam. They noted how efficiently and professionally Sam did the job. Before leaving work that day Maleep purchased a bag of Skittles and, along with a gift card, wrote a personal note and stuck it on the candy:

> Hey Sam,
>
> Just saying thanks for the great customer reply we got from the WellCo job. You nailed it with skill and awesome service, making us all look good as a result. I appreciate you.
>
> Maleep

Maleep placed the gift on the driver's seat of Sam's service truck so it would be discovered first thing in the morning when Sam started their route. At the end of the following day, Maleep was in the office when there was a slight knock on the door. It was Sam (who never came into that area as a rule). Maleep looked up and smiled. In a shy, humble voice, while looking at the floor, Sam muttered, "Hey, thanks dude. That was cool," and promptly turned and left.

From that moment the relationship between Sam and Maleep took on a new dimension. Sam never became a team engagement champion, but a personalized Reward token as small as it seemed made a positive difference in their relationship going forward. This concept needs to be the theme when providing any tangible Reward. Large or small, it may unknowingly play a crucial part for an employee to help balance the weight of their 3-R scale. Establishing an individual relationship with each employee to provide personalized Rewards is another step toward understanding the new employee engagement experience.

ORGANIZATIONS CAN PERSONALIZE REWARDS TOO

Organizations are also rethinking how to infuse more personalization and flexibility in company-provided Reward options particularly when it comes to employee benefits and offering à la carte options. There is a move toward setting up individual employee perk accounts where credits are deposited and can be spent on any combination of preapproved expenses such as healthcare premiums, additional home office equipment, student loan payments, childcare, commuting, to name a few examples.

It's interesting to see just how many employees are willing to give up a Reward in exchange for reducing the Requirements weight. For example, GoodHire recently found that 61% of survey respondents would be willing to take a pay cut to maintain their remote working option. Seventy percent of those surveyed also said that they would forfeit Rewards like health insurance benefits, paid time off, and retirement accounts to keep working remotely.

WE CAN'T COMPETE WITH THAT!

Because of limited resources or regulations, small businesses, government agencies, and public sectors may feel they can't compete with large corporations in providing the same range of Rewards or ad hoc incentives. Perhaps, but that doesn't mean they can't provide Rewards that are just as personalized and meaningful to individual employees.

Companies that aren't able to provide stock options, healthcare coverage, or retirement plans may be able to offer additional training, growth opportunities, ability to gain new certifications, upskilling, reskilling, succession planning visibility, mentoring opportunities, or special project assignments for personal growth and development.

Many top performers prefer to join small businesses, government agencies, and nonprofits just for the causes they represent or the opportunity for more autonomy, growth, and immediate control of their future. Top performers thrive on new opportunities and experiences.

Small organizations can keep top performers engaged by letting them learn the business by shadowing their leader for a week and allowing regular opportunities to work directly with the owner of a small business. If you think that you can't provide monetary incentives to compete with attracting and retaining top talent, think wider, get more creative with what you can provide. Even the way a paycheck is distributed can be an additional Reward. Companies realize that for some employees being paid every two weeks creates a hardship to pay bills as they come due and are offering a pay-every-day or weekly option.

There are plenty of people looking for many more different types of Rewards than the traditional ones—fulfillment and higher purpose to name two. As with determining the weight of the Requirements, people leaders won't know what their employees will truly value as a Reward unless they ask.

HAVE A 3-R REWARDS CONVERSATION

The most effective leaders with the highest employee retention rates clearly define meaningful Rewards for each employee even beginning with the onboarding process. If they inherit a team, it becomes one of the first conversations in getting to know each member reporting to them. It is imperative for people leaders to have a Reward conversation with each of their people and get answers to these questions:

- How do you define a Reward?

- Make a list of all the tangible rewards you currently receive at work. How would you rank them in priority from most value to least valuable for you?

- What is missing from the current Rewards you receive?

- If you had an extra $25, how would you spend it on yourself?

- How do you like to receive praise and recognition?

- Who do you most prefer to be recognized by?

- How are your peers doing in giving you merited recognition?

- Do you prefer public or private recognition?

- What type of written recognition do you prefer?

- What are your favorite hobbies/leisure time activities?

- What are your favorite book genre/color/fast-food/treats?

In the initial Rewards conversation, start with a list of extrinsic Reward examples available in your organization for the employee to review, add to, delete, and prioritize.

Tangible Reward Examples

- Backpacks
- Bonuses
- Bring pet/child to work
- Cards/thank-you notes
- Certifications
- Chair massages
- Coffee/teas
- Community volunteer opportunities
- Company swag
- Continuing education credits
- Day care
- Development programs/create their own development plans
- Dining out
- Education reimbursement
- Engagement with key leaders
- Financial awards
- Gift cards
- Gym passes
- Hobby day
- Home office setup allowance
- Mentorship
- Movie/theater/concert tickets
- New/improved job title
- Paycheck
- Phone allowance
- Professional coach
- Sabbaticals
- Snacks
- Spa day
- Special projects
- Special recognition events
- Sporting events
- Tech gadgets
- Time off
- Training
- Transportation reimbursement
- Water bottles/sports gear
- Well-being resources

Meaningful Rewards are as unique as the individuals themselves. Employees want flexibility and choice to select what is most valuable to them. It's also important to ensure that Rewards are allocated fairly. There is a difference between treating everyone the same and treating them equitability.

TAKE FIVE

1. Meaningful Rewards are defined only by the person receiving them.

2. Financial Rewards will always play a part in an employee's decision to leave or stay if they sense any inequities in fairness.

3. Because people leaders and organizations may wrongly assume what an employee values as a Reward, there are many misses when it comes to handing them out.

4. Meaningful Rewards that carry a lot of weight can be anything from a token bag of candy to a significant cash award.

5. The most effective leaders with the highest employee retention rates clearly define meaningful Rewards for each employee even beginning with the onboarding process.

SURVIVAL TACTIC #1
HAVE A 3-R REWARDS CONVERSATION

Explore the term *Reward* with each of your employees to understand what is most meaningful to them. Rewards can be major such as compensation and health benefits, or minor as a personalized card or snack treat.

Begin the conversation: *Rewards are best when they are the most meaningful to the person receiving them. I want to be sure that the Rewards you are receiving are of the most value to you, as well as Rewards that you may receive in the future. Please complete the "Getting to Know You" worksheet.*

GETTING TO KNOW YOU

Team Member_____   Date_____

- Backpacks
- Bonuses
- Bring pet/child to work
- Cards/thank-you notes
- Certifications
- Chair massages
- Coffee/teas
- Community volunteer opportunities
- Company swag
- Continuing education credits
- Day care
- Development programs/create their own development plans
- Dining out
- Education reimbursement
- Engagement with key leaders
- Financial awards
- Gift cards
- Gym passes
- Hobby day
- Home office setup allowance
- Mentorship
- Movie/theater/concert tickets
- New/improved job title
- Paycheck
- Phone allowance
- Professional coach
- Sabbaticals
- Snacks
- Spa day
- Special projects
- Special recognition events
- Sporting events
- Tech gadgets
- Time off
- Training
- Transportation reimbursement
- Water bottles/sports gear
- Well-being resources

1. If you had an extra \$25, how would you spend it on yourself?

2. What are your favorite leisure activities? Hobbies?

3. Favorite color?

4. Favorite type of music?

5. Favorite reading genre?

6. Favorite snack food?

7. Favorite fast food?

8. Preferred way to be recognized? Publicly? Privately?

9. What other Reward would be most meaningful to you?

Make a list of the tangible rewards you currently receive. Rate them on a 1 to 5 scale.

(1)	(2)	(3)	(4)	(5)
No Value	Slight Value	Neutral	Substantial Value	Major Value

REWARDS	RATING 1-5

SURVIVAL TACTIC #2
TEAM MEMBER REWARD INVENTORY

Once you have each team member complete the Getting to Know You form, transfer the data to the Inventory Grid and track your Reward process:

MEMBER'S NAME	FAVORITE COLOR	HOBBY	FAST FOOD	SNACK FOOD	MUSIC	RECOGNITION PREFERENCES	REWARD NOTES/ DATES

10

RESPECT: HOW AM I FEELING WHILE DOING THIS JOB?

Any business that loses a top performer because of a lack of Respect from either the leader or the organization has two choices: quickly make it right or watch your people flee.

At this point there are now two weights hanging on the employee's 3-R scale. On one side are the Requirements and on the other side hang the Rewards. Hopefully the scale is initially in balance with the employee feeling that the Rewards they are getting in return are equal to the Requirements they are being asked to meet.

The scale, however, won't stay in balance for long until the final and perhaps most critical piece is added: Respect. When the Respect weight is added to the scale, it can either be the final tipping point in a decision to leave if it's too light or, if heavy enough, can be a major way to counterbalance the Requirements and sway the decision to stay.

Feeling respected on the job is one of the most powerful motivators of employee engagement and retention. So much so, it can go a long way in balancing the 3-R scale. In many cases Respect can outweigh Rewards. Especially since the pandemic, people are much more willing to give up some Rewards in exchange for a feeling of being respected.

According to a recent survey conducted by the Society for Human Resource Management, respectful treatment of all employees at all levels was rated as "very important" by 72% of employees surveyed, making it the top contributor to overall employee job satisfaction.

In a 2014 *Harvard Business Review* article by Christine Porath, studies proved just how powerful Respect can be. It was noted that being treated respectfully outweighed every other leader behavior in terms of importance to employees, more so than recognition, appreciation, communicating an inspiring vision, providing useful feedback—even opportunities for learning, growth, and development.

Respect also had a clear impact on engagement. The more Respect leaders gave, the higher the level of employee engagement: people who said leaders treated them with Respect were 55% more engaged.

Given the importance of Respect as a single factor that drives retention and the fact that it is free and available to all organizations no matter the industry, size, type, and availability of resources, you would think it would be lavishly spread around every workplace culture as a result. Yes, you would think.

Here's the bad news, over 54% of employees claimed that they don't regularly get Respect from their leader—which makes no sense, right? If feeling disrespected results in lower engagement, higher turnover, and detrimental impact to the business on all fronts, why do over half of employees feel so disrespected? The excuses are shallow, but they are unfortunately real.

Many studies have followed up with leaders who scored low in the Respect area on 360 Surveys, where feedback on their leadership approach is provided by several different levels of employees they impact. Two of the primary explanations offered for the low Respect scores included feeling stressed and pressured with no time to be nice (as if being respectful is an extra demand on time) and no positive role models—they were just emulating the behavior they saw in their own leader. Ouch.

It's worthy to note that the reasons for being disrespectful are not so much intentional as they are from a lack of self-awareness of one's impact on others. So before we talk about how employees will personalize and differently define indicators of Respect, let's first stop and make sure you are not in that 54% of leaders that employees are calling disrespectful.

QUICK TIPS FOR CREATING A CULTURE OF RESPECT

- **Be the first to model respect.** Don't make Respect conditional. If you are withholding Respect because you're not receiving it, break the cycle. Take the high road as the leader and model what you want to see in others regardless of how you may be treated.

- **Nip disrespect in the bud.** The more you tolerate disrespectful behavior, the more you are training your team to be so. They are going to model what they see you do and allow, not what you say. Don't allow disrespect to happen. Take the person aside and respectfully let them know that the behavior you observed is not acceptable.

- **Hire for respectability.** Candidates may be top result winners, but at what cost? When doing reference checks, ask about how they treated others they worked with.

- **Apologize.** Slips happen. We are human. If you find yourself in a less than respectful moment, acknowledge it and apologize. No egos here. Ask the team to help hold you accountable as well as each other for the standards of Respect you want supported.

THE MANY DEFINITIONS OF RESPECT

The definition of the word *respect* is subjective—just as in telling someone they are rude or disrespectful may likely result in a defensive response of, "No, I'm not." Parents know this fact all too well when instructing a three-year-old to be good while in the grocery store. The adult definition of good means to stay in your seat and keep hands to yourself. While the kid interpretation of being good means it's okay to hurl the sippy cup at the person coming toward you as long as you stay seated in the cart and don't touch them. The behaviors can range widely based on an individual's interpretation of the word, the same way Respect behaviors can be misinterpreted in the workplace.

We're not talking about basic human civility here. It's never appropriate to swear at someone, call them names, degrade them in any way, bully, or embarrass them. Those are givens. But Respect wires can sometimes get crossed as in the case of the following scenario.

It's Friday afternoon. Finley, the team leader, sends an email to Desta, a top performer on the team, requesting additional information to complete a presentation for Monday morning. Finley is going out of town for the weekend and needs the data to complete the presentation before the day's end.

In top performer fashion, Desta drops everything to ensure Finley has what is needed and sends back the information within the time requested. It's now the end of the day and Desta closes down for the weekend. Having received no return email or text from Finley acknowledging the work, Desta is left to assume that the information was received as requested and all expectations met. While on the drive home with still no communication from Finley, Desta starts feeling a bit miffed, somewhat unappreciated, and slightly disrespected.

Finley's side of the story is a different perspective. Desta's information was precisely what was needed, and the presentation was finished at 7:00 p.m. Before taking off, Finley was about to send a quick acknowledgment to Desta but, realizing the hour and out of respect for Desta's personal time, ended up deleting it so as not to add another "ping from the boss" or email to an already overflowing inbox. Same incident, two people, and completely different definitions of Respect.

As with the Requirements of the job and a valued Reward for doing the job, Respect is subject to each person's independent weighting system. People leaders must ask and understand how an individual will define Respect. A leader cannot show Respect by second-guessing what it looks like for the individual person or, worse, demonstrating it in a way they would define for themselves. In the following scenario for example, Jessie, a team leader, experienced first-hand how differently the definitions of Respect could be played out among different team members.

As part of the initial onboarding meeting with each team member, Jessie always included this question, *Beyond basic civility (no bullying, profanity, and so on), what does Respect look like for you in terms of your communication preferences, preferred interaction styles, and boundaries as we establish our working relationship together?* The individual responses Jessie received from two different employees were revealing.

The first team member replied, *Since I'm fairly new to the industry and have a lot to learn, I would appreciate some extra time with you in addition to our scheduled weekly 1:1 meetings. Maybe we could do a daily five- to ten-minute check—just for the first couple of months so I can ask questions and make sure I'm on the right track with my projects and decisions. Your time and availability would be huge to me in terms of respecting my need for additional support as I ramp up. Feeling super supported is one way I define Respect.*

The second team member replied, *The best way you can demonstrate Respect toward me is to ensure the expectations you have for my project deliverables are clear and prioritized. Then, please just let me fly. We can connect as needed between our 1:1s, but my worst nightmare is being micromanaged.*

The result is two completely different definitions of Respect and a significant risk for the leader to miss the mark with both of them by not asking the right questions. When people leaders don't clarify an individual's meaning of respectful behaviors, the default position is to treat people the way they themselves want to be treated. That approach works well if all team members' Respect criteria align with the leader's, which is hardly the case.

When a people leader demonstrates Respect that fits the employee's definition, it becomes a compelling intrinsic reward. The person feels appreciated, empowered, and valued for the individual they are. Decades of research show the positive correlation between Respect and intrinsic motivation that drives an employee's feelings of autonomy and competence in their abilities. When combined with the right level of challenge and achievement, these feelings ultimately translate into a sense of fulfillment and purpose.

HAVE A 3-R RESPECT CONVERSATION

A leader can demonstrate Respect in several categories. For each of the following categories it will be helpful to ask individual employees to define their preferences. For example, with communication, ask, "What communication vehicle is the most effective for you? Do you prefer email, text, phone call, or Slack board post? I want to make sure whatever communication channel we use works best for you so that we have acknowledgment/replies with each other as needed, within one business day."

Another example to demonstrate Respect is clarifying their preferred working environment: "Tell me about the environments where you do your best work. How would you structure an ideal workweek as a result? What days would you elect to be on-site, remote, work from home, work from another site? What does a combination of those options look like for you?"

If working offsite is not an option as in the retail, hospitality, or food service industries, Respect can still be generated with a question like, "What works best for you with scheduling these next two workweeks? Is there a day/time that you prefer to come in/not come in. Is there a better part of the day for you to get certain tasks done?"

The point here, perhaps more so than the actual question being asked, is in the spirit of the asking. It's unreasonable to think that every employee's preference for shifts, days off, or days on, or communication vehicles will be accommodated upon every request. But the most important aspect is that the leader is asking the question and seeking to understand what set of circumstances is needed for a collaborative working arrangement that can be designed to meet everyone's needs. Even a little Respect in the asking with an earnest attempt to fulfill the requests can speak volumes to the Respect weight of their 3-R scale.

Carefully review the following chart of Respect categories for the areas you can clarify for each of the employees on the team. In addition to communication and environment, maybe start with how you will both meet. How frequently? In what format? In a remote setting does the employee prefer camera on or off? The more you ask, the more you seek to serve, the more Respect weight will be added.

AREAS TO CLARIFY FOR PERSONALIZING RESPECT

CATEGORY	CUSTOMIZATION
Leader interactions	• Behaviors that demonstrate Respect
Communication	• Preference: email, text, phone, team boards • Expected response times: within twenty-four hours, on/off business hours • Personal space
Meetings	• Frequency: 1:1s, team meetings, project meetings • Format: face-to-face, virtual, phone • Attendance: what meetings are high payoff/low payoff
Environment	• Location: on-site, remote, combination of office and remote • Preference: noise, privacy, collaboration

CATEGORY	CUSTOMIZATION
Level of autonomy	• What does that look like? • Too much? Too little?
Projects	• Preference: content, visibility • Interaction: team/individual
Learning	• Personal growth: parameters/limitations • Preference: desired experiences
Social interaction	• Preference: introvert/extravert • Activities
Mental well-being	• Priorities • Description

Having ongoing conversations around each of these categories will help to clarify how an employee defines Respect. While every preference will not necessarily be met, such as an employee's potential desire for "no 1:1 meetings," leaders can at least set the basics and work from there. Holding regular 1:1 meetings with each employee should be a nonnegotiable, but as long as the necessary information is effectively exchanged, does it matter how it's done? Holding the meeting in a way that's most preferred by the employee can be a highly valued demonstration of Respect.

Attendance at meetings is another way Respect is manifested. Everyone knows too well the drain and counterproductivity that back-to-back, low payoff meetings have on the Respect of an individual's time. Being present only to be privy to information without adding benefit is not a justifiable use of time if the information is accessible another way. Unless a team member serves an active role and provides specific value, there should be an allowance for a respectful decline. More employees in the name of mental wellness are already doing this by asking to preview the meeting agenda and clarifying the intent of their attendance before accepting the invitation.

Choices in one's working environment where possible is currently an essential factor in the Respect arena. Workplace choices and flexibility are already at the top of the strategic planning list for a company that expects to survive and is a key driver of employee retention. It's important for leaders to adopt a mindset of seeking ways to provide flexibility even in cases where it may not appear to do so. For example, if working from home 100% is not an option, can people's shifts be rotated to accommodate different stop/start times on certain days? Can they have any control in designing their own weekly schedules? Can any of the job tasks be completed remotely? Are the choices for paid time off and benefits dictated by a one-size-fits-all policy or allocated by personal needs?

The more creative an organization can be in providing flexibility and choices, the better the opportunities of attracting and keeping the best people.

Other avenues for demonstrating Respect, such as the desired level of autonomy, projects, learning, social interaction needs, and mental well-being descriptors, need to be discussed and customized. These areas may have contingencies that need to be clarified. For example, an employee may require a higher level of autonomy on a project in a familiar area but a much lower level if the content is new or the people are unknown.

The Respect weight on an employee's balance scale can make or break their decision to stay or leave. Conversations about defining Respect must be ongoing. Worse than not asking the questions necessary for balancing Respect is to collect the information and then disrespect the employee by ignoring the responses.

FEELINGS: THE UNIVERSAL DEFINITION OF RESPECT

The famous author Maya Angelou is quoted as saying, "I've learned that people will forget what you said, people will forget what you did, but people will never forget how you made them feel." This wise observation of human behavior is especially true when it comes to demonstrating Respect to employees. Feelings can be potent drivers for making choices. The degree a people leader exhibits the skill and will to demonstrate Respect in the most meaningful way to an individual employee will result in either the retention of the best and brightest workers or a churning mill of endless rotation. Respect alone is *that* powerful, and the stakes to get it right have never been higher.

Employers are being stretched in new ways to create processes and programs employees need, not what the organization thinks is required. When courting a valued new hire, the proclamation of "here's what we offer" is falling fast to "what do you need?" The employer/employee relationship has quickly transitioned away from the old command and control approach to a transparent arrangement that holistically meets the needs of both the employee and the organization.

Respect is 100% free. There are no excuses. Any business that loses a top performer because of a lack of respect has two choices: quickly make it right or watch your people flee. Today, top performers are calling the shots on this one and won't stand for anything less than feeling valued and respected in the workplace.

TAKE FIVE

1. Respect is one of the most powerful drivers in the 3-R scale with a major impact on retention. There are no excuses for not providing it as a people leader and as an organization. Respect is absolutely free.

2. When a people leader demonstrates Respect that fits the employee's definition, it becomes a compelling intrinsic reward. The employee feels appreciated, empowered, and valued for the individual they are.

3. When people leaders don't clarify an individual's meaning of respectful behaviors, the default position is to treat people the way they themselves want to be treated. And the greater the risk of being out of alignment with what your employee needs from you as their leader.

4. The Respect weight on an employee's 3-R scale can make or break their decision to stay or leave. Conversations about defining Respect must be ongoing. Worse than not asking the questions necessary for balancing Respect is to collect the information and then disrespect the employee by ignoring the responses.

5. There are no excuses. Respect is 100% free. There are no excuses. Any business that loses a top performer because of a lack of has two choices: quickly make it right or watch your people flee.

SURVIVAL TACTIC
HAVE A 3-R RESPECT CONVERSATION

As with Rewards, it's equally important to have individual employees define what Respect means in their work setting, especially in the relationship with their leader.

Begin the conversation: *Just as with Rewards, it's important to define Respect. Apart from human civility, Respect can look different to the person receiving it. I want to be sure that the way we engage is supporting your definition of Respect. For example, ways that we communicate, conduct meetings, honor personal space, set boundaries, and manage each other's expectations, let's look at these examples and see if there's anything that needs to be customized for you.*

Discuss the Respect Definitions worksheet with each team member to establish guidelines for demonstrating respectful behavior in a way that is meaningful for both of you. Clarify any customized preferences and note, for example, what is this team member's preferred communication vehicle? Are there personal boundaries of sending messages after work hours? What is the expected response time?

What does autonomy look like for each team member? When can you be too hands-on or too hands-off? The more you clarify each other's expectations and definitions of respect, the more successfully you can increase the Respect weight on their 3-R scale with activities that are most meaningful.

RESPECT DEFINITIONS

Team Member_____   Date_____

TYPE	DESCRIPTION	YOUR THOUGHTS/ PREFERENCES
Leader interactions	• Behaviors that demonstrate Respect	
Communication	• Email, text, phone, team boards • Expected response times: within twenty-four hours, on/off business hours • Personal space	
Meetings	• Frequency: 1:1s, team meetings, project meetings • Format: face-to-face, virtual, phone • Attendance: what meetings are high payoff/low payoff	
Environment	• Location: on-site, remote, combination of office and remote • Preference: noise, privacy, collaboration	
Level of autonomy	• What does that look like? • Too much? Too little?	
Projects	• Preference: content, visibility • Interaction: team/individual	
Learning	• Personal growth: parameters/limitations • Preference: desired experience	
Social interaction	• Preference: introvert/extravert • Activities	
Mental well-being	• Priorities • Description	

11

IT ALL HANGS IN THE BALANCE

Whether an employee chooses to stay or leave an organization comes down to a simple balancing act. If the Requirements balance with the Rewards and Respect, they will stay. If there's no balance, employees leave.

Now that you have an overview of the 3-R scale with a background on what makes up each of the Requirements, Rewards, and Respect weights, as well as how employees will personalize the impact of each, it's time for the fine balancing act to begin. There are four possible outcomes in how the combined weight of the Rewards and Respect will potentially balance the weight of the Requirements and ultimately affect a decision of an employee to leave or stay.

OUTCOME #1: BALANCED

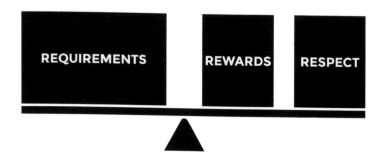

Outcome #1 depicts an employee's 3-R scale that is ideally balanced. The Requirements, Rewards, and Respect are aligned. This is the ideal outcome with the highest probability that your employee, especially a top performer, will happily stay. This perfectly balanced scale meets the needs of the employee as well as the organization, resulting in a high level of engagement and productivity.

As long as this balance is maintained, the satisfied employee will be thinking, *I enjoy working hard, doing my best work, and I am content with the meaningful Rewards I'm getting in return. I look forward to going to work. My leader is supportive and respectful and keeps me challenged with growth opportunities. I feel satisfied, appreciated, valued, and fulfilled. I love my job.*

OUTCOME #2: RESPECT IS TOO LIGHT

In outcome #2 the employee's 3-R scale is out of balance because the Respect is too light. There are three ways to create balance:

1. Increase Respect to at least match Rewards.
2. Further increase Rewards to outweigh Requirements.
3. Decrease Requirements.

This 3-R scale represents a flight risk situation. It's also safe to assume this employee will expend a minimal amount of effort and produce less than a high quality of work.

Unless the Rewards weight is continuously increased to make up for the lack of Respect, this person will leave for another opportunity as soon as it comes along. Their thinking is something like this: *The money and other Rewards I'm getting are awesome, but they treat me horribly. I don't like working here, but I'm kind of trapped. Where am I going to go and make this kind of money? And I need to keep the healthcare coverage for my family. For now, guess I'll keep sucking it up until something better comes along.*

Needless to say, they are not fulfilled, satisfied, or engaged and how tragic if it's happening to a once top performer.

OUTCOME #3: REWARDS ARE TOO LIGHT

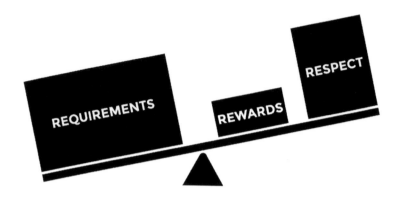

In outcome #3 the employee's 3-R scale is out of balance because Rewards are too light. There are three ways to create balance:

1. Increase Rewards to at least match Respect.
2. Further increase Respect to outweigh Requirements.
3. Decrease Requirements.

This represents a situation that small businesses, startups, government agencies, and public sectors may contend with when perhaps the initial Rewards weight can't be made as heavy by offering the numerous attractive perks and benefits larger organizations can. Many of the so-called high glam–low pay positions fall into this category where the fun of doing the job far outweighs the compensation and other Rewards in return.

Interestingly this scenario is recently gaining in popularity as employees reevaluate their life goals and prioritize what's important. Since the pandemic, millions of people have left high Reward positions in search of jobs that will provide more personal fulfillment and degree of Respect for them as human beings by fueling their mental well-being and desire for a higher purpose.

The important point for keeping employees is the impact of Respect. Organizations that double-down in that part of the 3-R scale stand a better chance to keep their people, unless something changes in the employee's life. In that regard, they are still a flight risk albeit maybe not as strong as when the imbalance results from the Respect weight being lighter than the Rewards.

In this situation, the employee is thinking, *I'm not immediately going to get rich on this job, and I need to keep my barista gig on Saturdays, but I love working here. My leader treats me like gold and the people are the best coworkers I've ever worked with. I get to grow and do projects I love and in the way I need to get them done. I've never felt so at peace lately. The environment works best for my family and me. For the first time in my life, I wake up and want to go to work.*

OUTCOME #4: REWARDS AND RESPECT ARE TOO LIGHT

This is the Great Resignation sitting on a 3-R scale. Unfortunately it has been all too common in many organizations. It doesn't take much commentary to assess what is going on here. It's a matter of how quickly the employee will leave, not if. Scenarios like this tend to deteriorate into this outcome over time. It would be a bit challenging to hire for this position right out the gate; it's more a case of a slow death by one drip at a time.

The job innocently starts with more and more work being added to the existing Requirements—drip. Nothing is added to the Rewards to make up for the additional weight plopped onto the Requirements— drip, drip. And the lack of Respect on top of it all creates an erosion of psychological safety—drip, drip, done.

DO GENERATIONS MATTER WHEN BALANCING A 3-R SCALE?

The fact that people are *people* first and generationally different second gives us the first indicator to answer the question about whether generations matter when it comes to balancing a 3-R scale? Basic human needs will always be foundational; physiological needs, safety, love, belonging, self-esteem, and self-actualization are the primary drivers behind what ultimately motivates behavior regardless of age or any other characteristic.

That being said, there are additional nuances when it comes to the different weightings different generations may assign to the Rewards they value and the ways they would define Respect. The following chart provides a helpful guide in discussing potential Rewards and Respect needs with employees in each of the four generations currently working together today:

GENERATION	BORN	REWARDS	RESPECT
Baby Boomers	1946 – 1964	In-person events, award ceremonies, promotions, commemorative plaques, certificates, retirement planning, wellness programs, money, coaching/mentoring others	Theme: *I am valued and needed.* In-person meetings, human touch communications, friendliness, acknowledgment of loyalty, appreciate their life experiences
Gen X	1965 – 1980	Eldercare, private recognition, travel perks, delivery services, healthcare services, time off, professional development opportunities	Theme: *I prefer to do it my own way, forget the rules.* Opportunities to work in teams, collaboration, flexibility, autonomy
Millennials	1981 – 1996	Event tickets, classes, time off to volunteer, experiences, promotion through earned achievements, flexibility, scheduling freedom	Theme: *I want to work with other bright, creative people.* Feedback, being mentored, value lifestyle balance over upward mobility
Gen Z	1997 – 2012	Flexibility, work environment freedom, virtual/hybrid options, student loan repayment, want respect over any office perk	Theme: *My individual work matters to the team's success.* Short communication via devices and apps, frequent 1:1 meetings, diversity

BEWARE OF GENERATION BIAS

The research on generational differences confirms that although individual people may experience changes in their values and preferences over their professional lives, major differences due to age or generation alone don't appear to be supported. What seems to be the case, however, is the projection of age-bias behaviors resulting in the stereotyping of different groups.

Stereotypes of older workers include their being dependable, loyal, hard working, and responsible on the positive side, and stubborn, out-of-touch, and low-tech on the negative. Younger groups tend to be pegged as transparent, diverse, and collaborative, as well as unmotivated, entitled, or irresponsible. The interesting data point is that both older and younger workers believe others view them more negatively than they actually do, confirming that neither age-related stereotypes nor meta-stereotypes are accurate.

People leaders can leverage generational differences by keeping the team focused on goals they have in common and welcome the valued perspectives and contributions each generation can make. People leaders will also benefit from acknowledging that people are people first and employees second and will have more in common as human beings than generational differences.

Not every employee within the same age group will have the same experiences at the same exact time. Therefore, engaging in an ongoing and open dialogue with employees to discuss shifting needs to balance the Requirements with the Rewards and the Respect at any particular time is the real key to keeping top-performing employees engaged, happy, and productive with all their generational coworkers.

TAKE FIVE

1. There are four outcomes of a 3-R scale that will create various levels of potential turnover. Outcome #1 is the most favorable, when the weight of the Requirements is balanced with the combined weight of the Rewards and Respect generated in return. Employees are highly satisfied in this scenario and are the most likely to stay.

2. Outcome #2 reflects a 3-R scale that is out of balance because the Respect is too light and creates a tilt toward the Requirements side. This employee is a flight risk. Resenting the need to keep the job because of money or needed healthcare, their engagement and productivity will likely be lower as a result.

3. Outcome #3 shows a 3-R scale that is out of balance because the Rewards weight is too light, again tilting the scale to the Requirements side. This employee is also a flight risk if another opportunity comes along with the same weight of Respect, but with additional Rewards as well.

4. Outcome #4 is the worst scenario and unless corrected will result in high turnover. Both the Rewards and the Respect are too light to offset the weight of the Requirements. This condition usually doesn't happen overnight but is a result of leadership neglect over time.

5. While there are some minor nuances in the definition of Rewards and Respect among different generations, as human beings first, the basic need for safety, belonging, self-esteem, and self-actualization will be more powerful drivers and are universal to all regardless of age.

SURVIVAL TACTIC #1
BALANCE YOUR OWN 3-R SCALE

Part 1: Think about your own job and how it plays across each of the 3-Rs: Complete the table for your current position. Directly following this activity sheet is Survival Tactic #2 which has been designed for each of your team members to complete and discuss their own 3-R scale balance with you.

REQUIREMENTS	REWARDS	RESPECT
In the order of impact, list the direct and indirect Requirements you must meet to succeed at your job. (Review chapter 8 for a detailed explanation and sample list of Requirements.)	In the order of value, list the Rewards being received or are missing in return for doing this job. (Review chapter 9 for a detailed explanation and sample list of Rewards.)	In the order of value, list the behaviors being demonstrated or missing that demonstrate Respect for the work you do. (Review chapter 10 for a detailed explanation and sample of customized areas of Respect.)
Direct	Rewards I'm Receiving	Respect I'm Receiving
Indirect	Rewards I'm Missing	Respect I'm Missing

Part 2: Share your lists of the Requirements, Rewards, and Respect with your own leader. Together, review the following questions to determine any next steps needed to balance your own 3-R scale. (See chapter 12 for reference.)

1. How does the weight of the Requirements compare to the weight of the Rewards you are receiving in return? Circle one:

   A. The Requirements are equal to the Rewards. (Proceed to question 2.)

   B. The Requirements are heavier than the Rewards. Answer the following questions:

      - In what ways could the weight of the Requirements be decreased?

      - In what ways could the Rewards be increased to balance the Requirements?

2. How does the weight of the Requirements compare to the weight of the Respect you are receiving in return? Circle one:

   A. The Requirements are equal to the Respect. (Proceed to question 3.)

   B. The Requirements are heavier than the Respect. Answer the following question:

      - In what ways could the Respect be increased to balance the Requirements?

3. Consider the combined weight of the Rewards and the Respect. Is your 3-R scale in balance? How can you keep it that way? Do you anticipate any changes?

   Can the combination of the Rewards and Respect be adjusted together in order to meet the weight of the Requirements? For example, is there something that can be added to the Respect weight that would decrease the need for an additional Reward?

SURVIVAL TACTIC #2
TEAM MEMBER 3-R SCALE

Team Member_____   Date_____

Part 1: Think about your current job and how it breaks down into each of the 3-Rs: Requirements, Rewards, Respect.

REQUIREMENTS	REWARDS	RESPECT
In the order of impact, list the direct and indirect Requirements you must meet to succeed at your job. (Review Chapter 8 for a detailed explanation and sample list of Requirements.)	In the order of value, list the Rewards being received or are missing in return for doing this job. (Review Chapter 9 for a detailed explanation and sample list of Rewards.)	In the order of value, list the behaviors being demonstrated or missing that demonstrate Respect for the work you do. (Review Chapter 10 for a detailed explanation and sample of customized areas of Respect.)
Direct	Rewards I'm Receiving	Respect I'm Receiving
Indirect	Rewards I'm Missing	Respect I'm Missing

3-R SCALE BALANCE QUESTIONS

Team Member_____   Date_____

Part 2: Share your lists of the Requirements, Rewards, and Respect with your leader. Together, review the following questions to determine any next steps needed to balance your 3-R scale. (See chapter 12 for reference.)

1. How does the weight of the Requirements compare to the weight of the Rewards you are receiving in return? Circle one:

   A. The Requirements are equal to the Rewards. (Proceed to question 2.)

   B. The Requirements are heavier than the Rewards. Answer the following questions:

      • In what ways could the weight of the Requirements be decreased?

      • In what ways could the Rewards be increased to balance the Requirements?

2. How does the weight of the Requirements compare to the weight of the Respect you are receiving in return? Circle one:

   A. The Requirements are equal to the Respect. (Proceed to question 3.)

   B. The Requirements are heavier than the Respect. Answer the following question.

      • In what ways could the Respect be increased to balance the Requirements?

3. Consider the combined weight of the Rewards and the Respect. Is your 3-R scale in balance? How can you keep it that way? Do you anticipate any changes?

Consider the combined weight of the Rewards and Respect. Can they be adjusted together in order to meet the weight of the Requirements? For example, is there something that can be added to the Respect weight that would decrease the need for an additional Reward?

12

TILT! NOW WHAT?

Ensuring that employees have a balanced 3-R scale isn't just something nice to do if there's time. It's an imperative if any leader expects to keep a valued employee in this market.

It's a simple law of physics. To make an object heavier, you add weight. To make an object lighter, you subtract weight. Each of the Requirements, Rewards, and Respect weights can potentially be adjusted as needed to help balance a 3-R scale.

BEWARE OF SILENT REQUIREMENTS

Step one on the journey to adjusting the balance of a 3-R scale is to make sure you're not creating more work for yourself to begin with. Many 3-R scales start to break under the weight of the Requirements. This process doesn't typically happen overnight, and sometimes a leader as well as the organization is creating the problem by unconsciously adding weight to the Requirements. When additional Requirements pop up, they can be either loud or quiet.

Loud Requirements are in plain view and easily recognizable such as needing to build a relationship with a newly assigned team leader, having to learn a complex new inventory system, or absorbing the workload of a team member who just quit—all examples of prominent, visible changes to the Requirements. Everyone knows they're there and fully aware of their impact.

Silent Requirements are different from loud ones. They can creep up and are sneaky, taking root right under your nose. Those innocent, small requests especially of a top performer (because they are always so capable) don't happen in a vacuum or get absorbed into the atmosphere. They silently pile up on the Requirements side of their scale, and before you know it, even a crate of weightless feathers can get too heavy to lift.

Change fatigue is another silent Requirement not easy to recognize. Every action in the organization is going to create a reaction. Too many changes in too short a period of time becomes a stack of silent Requirements ready to scream, "TILT!" if no counterbalances are made to the Rewards and Respect side.

Be careful as well about designating your top performer as the team's go-to for questions and problem resolution. "Telling the team to 'Call 1-800 Top Performer' if you need help in—" is a not a wise retention strategy. Bottom line: beware of the many asks, that as stand-alones, don't seem like a big deal. Collectively they can wreak havoc with the Requirements weight of a 3-R scale, especially for your top performers

DECREASING THE REQUIREMENTS WEIGHT

Remember, before attempting to make weight adjustments to the Requirements, Rewards, and Respect, it's important to have first defined and clarified how each employee perceives the weight impact of each of them. You don't want to mistakenly lighten the Requirements by taking away something the employee didn't mind doing or even enjoyed.

And despite the best intentions, it won't be helpful to demonstrate a respectful behavior in the hopes of increasing the Respect weight, when the behavior is not one the employee finds especially valuable. So the best course of action is to always clarify which items making up the Requirements weight are the heaviest and how you can help lighten the load.

For example, many top performers dislike and get bogged down in the more mundane administrative tasks they must do in addition to their primary craft. Processing expense reports, filling out forms, and handling excessive paperwork are a few examples of administrative tasks that could be offloaded to other employees, interns, or entry-level employees who don't mind that type of work and may see it as a growth opportunity to learn about other parts of the business. Even a small monthly stipend to hire a virtual assistant a few hours a week would be helpful to free up your top talent to take additional challenging assignments they would welcome to fulfill their skill level and potential.

A recent survey in the *Harvard Business Review* noted that knowledge workers reported spending over 41% of their time on low-skilled tasks that did not require authority or expertise. Lightening this weight on their scale may go a long way in balancing it.

As noted, top performers can too easily become the team's go-to resource. They can get bombarded with questions on solving issues, requests for help on projects, and be held accountable for a new member's onboarding and training and become an unspoken mentor for advice on various topics. Lighten this Requirement by ensuring there is some sort of knowledge management system in place. Even an online community board where everyone has access to FAQs in a particular area will help. Spread the knowledge wealth among the team. In addition to the top performers being the automatic team gurus, assign a topic to everyone on the team to be the expert of their own area.

KEEP MEETINGS SHORT AND THE ATTENDEE LIST SHORTER

Back-to-back meetings are one of the biggest killers of productivity, the number one reason employees say they have no control over their workday, a primary driver of burnout, and the most common cause of adding unnecessary weight to the Requirements. Whew.

More than one top performer has lamented, "I spend more time meeting with my leader to tell them what I'm going to do, and then telling them what I did, than just doing the work itself."

So why are so many employees collapsing under the deluge of meetings? In some cases, it's the only way their leader knows how to disseminate information. For others, it may be a sense of false control—thinking, if I call a meeting, everyone will take proper note of the important information to be learned. People's meeting engagement bandwidth is already limited enough when sitting around a conference table in person, let alone adding a virtual mix of attendees to it.

Do what you can to ease the meeting pressure by asking the following questions before sending the next meeting invitation:

- What is the purpose of the meeting? Is it to inform? Collect decision-making input? If so, is there any other delivery vehicle that can achieve the same goal? Email? Message board?

- If there isn't another alternative, why is a meeting important? (Note that reason in the meeting invite.) If there isn't a reason, hold off until there is one.

- If there is a valid reason for the meeting, how will each person on the invite contribute to the reason for meeting? List what role each attendee will play as appropriate. If someone doesn't have a purposeful reason to contribute, exclude them from the invite.

- Keep the attendee list short (five to seven people) and the meeting time shorter (thirty minutes max). It's better to schedule two shorter meetings than one long one. Follow up with notes and post so others can access the information.

CREATE FLEXIBILITY IN SELECTING PROJECTS AND SCHEDULES

Because of their proven skill and initiative, top performers also tend to get the more difficult projects assigned to them. That's desirable if the assignment happens to be a project they like and want to work on. In that case it doesn't add to the Requirements and may even result in being a Reward. Instead of assigning projects, let employees choose a combination of projects they would find most enjoyable to work on, in addition to the occasional ones you need them to do.

People in general, especially top performers, tend to like variety in their work. Many employees can burn out from repetitive and monotonous tasks that do not challenge them. Top performers especially need inspiration to strive toward. They are constantly setting personal best goals for themselves and need a work environment that will allow them to pursue them. As possible, switch up their assignments to apply a variety of their many skills and talents.

For non-knowledge-worker–type positions, flexibility can still be considered in a number of ways. For example, adjust start and end times so they can accommodate different employees' scheduling needs. Create shorter shift bands perhaps with a rotation of duties and allow employees to select their own best options for the coming work period. Rethink overtime. Is it optional and flexible or rigid and mandatory? Watch for unconscious bleed into personal time without adding to the Requirements weights. Even a few minutes of "quick cleanup" resulting in routinely leaving fifteen minutes later than planned will creep up and sit heavily on their Requirements weight.

Another idea is to create a shift exchange process where employees are preapproved to work together and trade shifts that work best for them. Last, encourage them to use their time off as needed. Recognize their need for work-life balance and resist the hesitation to approve time off as soon as the pace calms down, which we all know it rarely does. It's understandable that working through these considerations has challenges, especially in union shops. Most business leaders know that some sort of flexible work arrangement is the right thing to do and must be part of their retention strategy. It will pay off in the long run to make even the smallest changes now.

PROVIDE OPPORTUNITIES FOR COLLABORATION

Some employees, especially Gen Zs and millennials are used to collaborating with others and enjoy working on team projects together. Many people at a top talent level welcome the growth and intellectual stimulation those opportunities provide. It gives them a high payoff for their work and a vital purpose for wanting to achieve it.

When paired with someone their equal, they will thrive on whatever can, in turn, potentially lighten the weight of the Requirements by providing a needed fulfillment of passion and growth when working with another talented colleague.

PROVIDE REMOTE WORKING OPTIONS

For millions of knowledge workers looking for their next employment move as well as for those thinking about staying with their current employer, working remotely is not an option; it's become mandatory and one of the most powerful counterbalances for the weight of the Requirements. According to a recent survey conducted by Bloomberg, over 40% of employees will refuse to stay or accept a new opportunity if working remotely in some capacity is not available. *Forbes* just completed a survey backed by Slack that showed 76% of knowledge workers want flexibility in their work, and 93% want flexibility in where they work.

The reasons driving this strong desire for remote work are widely varied—the most common being a need for better work-life balance. When it comes to the combination of on-site and remote preferences, employees are all over the board. Some want to be 100% remote, others completely on-site, and the rest want a combination of both on-site and offsite options, and with the added layer of working a varied week of optional hours at any time of the day.

What we do know for sure: providing flexible options where possible is the name of the game, and businesses not already on that bus are going to have a hard time attracting and keeping their people. Two-thirds of executives say their post-pandemic labor policies have little to no direct input from their employees. With the continuation of the highest quit rate in history, that may be a costly mistake.

RENOVATE THE JOB

A job is simply a collection of functions that are given to an employee to complete. Think about those tasks in the same way you might update a house. The end goal of creating a new living space doesn't change, but how the space is updated has a myriad of options. It's the same approach when considering how work gets done. The business goals and metrics of a particular job remain the same, but does the way those outcomes are achieved have to always stay the same as well?

When looking at process improvements, one of the key sources of information has always been to ask the people who are actually doing the job for their input. Not only do they feel valued and respected for their invited participation, but leaders can also gain many helpful insights. In addition, when those tasks can be realigned to an employee's strengths and skill sets, the Requirements weight lightens, and engagement is increased. When tasks are aligned to someone's talents and passions, work doesn't feel like work and employees will be more motivated to complete the tasks when they have a voice in saying how the job gets done.

One of the ways an organization can go about renovating a job is called crafting. Task crafting is the most common and consists of altering the type, scope, sequence, and number of tasks the employee is responsible for. Employees may take the initiative to change the way they carry out the tasks and their timing by electing to complete more strenuous or complicated tasks in the part of the day when their energy is at its highest.

Another type of job crafting is called relational crafting. Relational crafting refers to the control employees have over the people they interact with. Employees may choose the way and how frequently they will be required to connect with different coworkers. Engaging with colleagues takes more psychological energy for some, making the weight of their Requirements feel heavier; whereas, for others the opportunity to work with supportive and motivating employees is a welcome source of energy and inspiration.

Participation required in social events, work parties, or team outings may also be crafted. Employees may be required to attend some various functions, but optional activities like being assigned as a new hire's First-Day Buddy may be better left to someone else who has a natural talent for hospitality and welcomes that type of responsibility.

Finally, a job may be crafted cognitively. Cognitive crafting refers to the way an employee reshapes their perception of what they are doing to attach more meaning and self-fulfillment to their job. This is an intrinsic shift, but leaders can go a long way in helping employees reframe their thinking about what may be less-than-desirable mundane, low payoff tasks and how the potential of a bigger impact can be made.

SWIRLING IS THE NEW CORPORATE LADDER CLIMBING

The term "climbing the corporate ladder" refers to the steps of advancement employees may want to take to get to the top of the organization. Some companies can offer immensely tall ladders with multiple rungs on which to climb; others due to size may have only a few. In either case the ladder was typically vertical, offering one direction: up. Older work models of formal hierarchies where a more rigid chain of command structure was the norm provided few opportunities for advancement unless someone left or retired from their position.

Employees, especially top performers, end up quitting because of a lack of growth, inability to gain new experiences, and limited, if any, opportunities to develop new skills and advance, according to many surveys.

With the need to be more responsive and quickly solve business challenges in a fast-paced, competitive environment, many organizations moved to flatter and leaner organizational structures. Project teams became more the norm on how work gets done. As a result, there is a need to rethink ways to keep top performers who become quickly bored and need the next new challenge. Lateral movement up, down, and across, or *swirling* within an organization can help meet that need.

Swirling means motion. It's movement of any kind and not specifically in an intentional vertical line upward. When top performers are allowed the freedom to swirl by crossing departmental lines to take on meaningful projects and form new strategic relationships with key business partners, they can contribute their skills in multiple places. This movement, in turn, creates a strong sense of being valued and engaged.

Swirling can include opportunities like shadowing/interning with a senior leader or small business owner, receiving a mentor or business coach, gaining increased visibility for working on special assignments, or participating in special leadership cohorts. Top performers welcome opportunities to share in strategic planning, creativity, and organizational development activities to broaden their sphere of influence, connect with leaders outside their department, and gain access to a broader stage for their ongoing aspirations.

DIVIDE THE WHOLE INTO SMALLER PIECES

Perception can be everything when the size of job Requirements is undertaken. Upon first glance a goal may be daunting, but when broken into smaller, more manageable steps, it becomes quite attainable. While it may not always be doable or practical to remove tasks and specific job Requirements from an employee's 3-R scale, it is worth looking at how the perception of meeting those job metrics may be restructured.

For example, the aggressive goal of reducing lab reporting delay times by 68% over the next three months may feel unduly heavy sitting on the Requirements side of the scale, with lots of moving parts and lack of clarity on exactly how to go about it. Instead, by breaking down each of the steps and creating a sequence of events needed, people can more clearly see a smaller goal they can directly impact and thus create the perception of a lighter Requirements weight. If lab result delays are partly due to incorrect email or home addresses, the team updating that information can more likely rally behind a smaller goal of focusing on the timely delivery of updating the database.

Another example: cleaning out an overwhelmingly messy bedroom will be more successful by first setting a goal of clearing out and organizing what's under the bed, or just in one drawer, or the closet. Perception can be everything when it comes to motivation and feeling a heavier weight of the job's Requirements.

The main point about assessing the weight of the job's Requirements is to consider how it can be lightened in the eyes of the individual doing the work. The most important part is to have honest and frequent conversations about the Requirements and any possible ways the perceived weight can be made less burdensome. And remember that life can change for any employee in a moment. New circumstances may positively or negatively impact them in a way that was different from the previous week, supporting the need to have ongoing conversations about the Requirements as a key part in maintaining balance of their 3-R scale.

INCREASING THE REWARDS WEIGHT

While the goal of adjusting the Requirements weight is to provide a sense of lightening the workload, the opposite occurs for adjusting the Rewards and the Respect weight. Here we want to increase their weight as a counterbalance for the Requirements. When it comes to adding weight to the Rewards, remember the most important step is to first clarify with each employee how they define Rewards. People leaders can miscalculate the positive impact of a Reward by thinking because it's something they would desire, their people would too.

Harvard Business School Assistant Professor Ashley V. Whillans noted that more than 80% of American employees say they do not feel recognized or rewarded, even though US companies are spending more than one-fifth of their budgets on wages—further validation that leaders' actions are not landing with employees' expectations. More money, benefits, or perks, as we know, are not always equal motivators for everyone.

In addition to monetary types of Rewards, many helpful resources offer suggestions for nonmonetary Rewards. These may include occasionally reassigning a task an employee doesn't particularly enjoy, shadowing a coworker to learn more about the business, gaining new skills, being leader-for-a-day for those who want to advance, letting employees design and personalize their workstation, attending skip-level meetings with their leader's manager, or inviting them to join a panel that provides input on programs and policies.

Most importantly, ask each one of your people what matters most to each of them. The most crucial point is to remember a Reward is in the eyes of the beholder.

INCREASING THE RESPECT WEIGHT

It can't be said enough in today's work environment that one of the most repeated demands heard from employees is to be respected in ways most meaningful to them. One way a leader can start to universally increase employees' Respect weight is to adopt a spirit of gratitude. It's so easy to get caught up in looking at everything that needs correcting. How much of your day do you choose to look at what is going right and overtly recognize the people who are making it so?

Naturally grateful people are wonderful to be around, and employees want to work for them. People who aren't naturally grateful and always on the negative can soon become tiresome to be near, and if the ungrateful person happens to be the employee's leader, their 3-R scale is well on its way to tilt. Leaders don't lead with gratitude for many reasons, but, frankly, none of them matter.

Unspoken or not, employees have expectations for their leader to express gratitude and appreciation when their work warrants it. Examples include helping their leader with a significant task, going out of their way to assist a coworker, working late, contributing an idea, volunteering to do a task outside their job description, or taking on additional work without being asked. Too often leaders can overlook someone's initiative and efforts on a project or task if the outcomes don't match the expected results. There is always a positive to be gleaned even if it's no more than a lesson learned from a project that didn't meet its objectives. In addition to the celebratory fanfare provided when achieving high visibility goals, appreciation can significantly add to the Respect weight.

Leaders need to be on the lookout for the more subtle gestures done by an employee that indirectly contribute to the team's benefit. Perhaps without being asked, someone offered to take on extra tasks for the last thirty minutes of their shift so their coworker could make it to their child's soccer game across town. Or maybe the administrative assistant not only provided the sales report requested but took the initiative to color-code the product types to assess the data more quickly.

The more a leader looks for the opportunity to express appreciation and models gratitude, the heavier an employee's Respect weight will become. The adage, "people don't care how much you know until they know how much you care," is a potent reminder for leaders to think about how they can make this ring true for their people. To the degree a leader models gratitude, it permeates the team culture. As a result, coworkers also come from appreciation and look for opportunities to express Respect to each other. The more Respect that is generated among the team, the heavier the Respect weight becomes on everyone's 3-R scale.

A BALANCED SCALE IS MORE THAN JUST A NICE IDEA

Ensuring that employees have a balanced 3-R scale isn't just something nice to do if there's time. It's an imperative if any leader expects to keep a valued employee in this market. The delicate balance of work satisfaction is as dynamic as daily life, and an employee's scale must continuously be reviewed, discussed, and rebalanced as needed. The success and sustainability of any business is contingent on employees feeling engaged enough to show up and do the work. The pandemic has only served to intensify these needs.

People are reassessing what they ultimately want from life and view work as only one avenue to meet their life goals instead of as a primary source of validation and identity, as with so many employees in previous decades. The power shift of control from employer to employee has so drastically changed in the past couple of years. This shift is creating a whole new paradigm for companies to develop strategies that will not only attract top performers but engage and retain them, if not for a lifetime, at least for a time of substantial, long-term contributions.

Leaders must have specific and frequent conversations about their employees' 3-R scales and be willing to talk openly about the weights and potential changes needed to ensure the scales stay in balance. While balancing flexibility requests with the requirements of the business takes some finesse, it's more than worth risking the opposite of plowing ahead with a command and control approach where employees feel they are nothing more than robots with no control over what they do. Fulfilled, satisfied, and engaged employees will lead by example, especially when those employees are top performers. Others will see their success and will want to emulate them.

While structuring the perfect job for every employee may not be achievable, research confirms that an employee will outperform expectations if their tasks tap into their strengths and abilities. The most important aspect is that managers and employees have honest and frequent conversations about the Requirements and any possible ways the perceived weight can be less burdensome. Leaders coming from a servant leadership style do this intuitively. This approach is a natural part of their relationship-building repertoire. They constantly assess their people's needs and remove roadblocks, thus freeing them up to exceed expectations with happiness and enthusiasm.

TAKE FIVE

1. Many 3-R scales start to tilt under the weight of the Requirements. This process doesn't typically happen overnight, and sometimes a leader as well as the organization is creating the problem by unconsciously adding weight to the Requirements.

2. Back-to-back meetings are one of the biggest killers of productivity. It's a primary reason employees say they have no control over their workday, why it's reported as a primary driver of burnout, and the most common cause of adding unnecessary weight to the Requirements. Only hold a meeting when there isn't a more optimal way to distribute the information.

3. Perception can be everything when the size of job Requirements is undertaken. Upon first glance a goal may be daunting, but when broken into smaller, more manageable steps, it becomes quite attainable.

4. When it comes to adding weight to the Rewards, remember the most important step is to first clarify with each employee how they define the word *reward*. People leaders can miscalculate the positive impact of a Reward by thinking because it's something they would desire, their people would too.

5. Change fatigue is another silent Requirement not easy to recognize. Every action in the organization is going to create a reaction. Too many changes in too short a period of time become a stack of silent Requirements ready to scream, "Tilt!" if no counterbalances are made to the Rewards and Respect.

SURVIVAL TACTIC #1
DECREASE THE REQUIREMENTS WEIGHT

When the Requirements weight is too heavy for the Rewards and Respect being generated in return, a place to begin balancing a 3-R scale is with lightening the Requirements. Be as creative as possible. Consider these questions:

- Are any silent Requirements adding hidden weight? Are top performers either consciously or unconsciously taking on small tasks, or being hampered with low-priority administrative work that can be consolidated or delegated?

- What's the status of the technology? Does it make sense to provide or upgrade collaboration tools to make team communication and information processing easier and more efficient? Are team members complaining about poor visibility into the system and access to data needed to do their jobs?

- Can you provide additional flexibility in scheduling options? Shift times? Adjustable start and stop times? Remote or hybrid options?

- Are there opportunities to provide more collaboration with others? Can team members work together to make any tasks less burdensome?

- Can the job be realigned to the employee's specific skills and talents? Are there other options for getting the work done but in a different way? Can an employee batch more difficult tasks and do them together in a way or at different times that work better for them?

- Are there any opportunities for the employee to gain a sense of more control over the work they are doing? Have you asked for their input?

SURVIVAL TACTIC #2
MAKE MEETINGS MORE EFFICIENT

Meetings are one of the biggest culprits in adding additional weight to the Requirements. How many meetings do you hold per week? Per month? Can any of them be consolidated or streamlined? Are all team members required to attend all meetings?

Before sending the next meeting invite, consider—

- What is the purpose of the meeting? (inform, make a decision, take action)

- Is there any other way the information can be provided? (email, message board)

- What is the best format to conduct the meeting? (virtual, in person, hybrid, standup/huddle, 1:1, project team)

- How will each attendee add value to the meeting?

- Have you provided a planned agenda, with the purpose and meeting goals?

MEETING PLANNER GUIDE

Use this guide to help keep the meeting on track.

MEETING PLANNER

Meeting Name:		Organizer:	
Date:			
Time:			
Location:			
Primary Goal for Meeting:			

Facilitator:	Attendees:		

Agenda Items			
Topic	Owner	Action	Next Steps

Notes

PART IV

BALANCED FROM THE BEGINNING

The most effective way to optimize a 3-R scale is to set it up as fully balanced as possible from the beginning. What's the beginning? Employees will have already started to hang the Requirements, Rewards, and Respect weights on their 3-R scale with the very first touch they have with the company. In most cases that means their recruiting experience and the ease of the application process and follow-up. Candidates and new hires will start adjusting weights during the interviewing process, their first day on the job, and their onboarding experience.

The impact of the true culture as new employees come to know it after the first few weeks on the job is a critical turning point in their decision to leave or stay. An unhealthy culture will cause what may be an uncorrectable tilt to their scale right out of the gate. Take note: one of the most crucial impacts to the early balance of their 3-R scale is the initial relationship with their leader.

This part of the book focuses on how a company's culture, recruiting process, onboarding experiences, and the behaviors of their people leaders can either make or break a 3-R scale from the beginning.

13

HOW CULTURE IMPACTS A 3-R SCALE

It's impossible not to have a culture. If a company doesn't care about their culture, not caring is the culture.

Culture drives everything a company does or does not do. It determines the recruiting process and the way a candidate is interviewed. Culture sets up the first-day-on-the-job experience, the onboarding process, and the all-important relationship with the leader. It's that ubiquitous force that shapes a company's policies and programs. It defines the way its members interact with one another and specifically what behaviors are tolerated from its people leaders.

Culture is the sum of the organization's attitudes and values and is best observed by what people actually do and not by what they say they would like to do. A company's culture is reflected by its dress code, business hours, office setup, hiring decisions, treatment of customers, employee satisfaction, and every other part of its operations. Even the tone of texts and emails that bounce back and forth are clear lenses into a company's culture. Culture is also a major force in successfully setting up a balanced 3-R scale.

If any scale is set upon a sloping or irregular surface, it will instantly tilt, so attempts to balance it will be challenging. If the foundation for the base of a scale is smooth, even, and supportive, the scale will stand upright and can easily be adjusted as weights are added and subtracted. If the foundation for the scale is filled with irregularities and heavily slanted to one side, the scale will instantly wobble making the balancing unnecessarily complex if not almost impossible.

Think of your company's culture as the base a 3-R scale will sit on. A smooth and supportive base will uphold employee retention. An irregular and inconsistent one will result in employee turnover. A recent study conducted by the Hays recruitment firm noted that almost half of the 2,100 employees surveyed said they were looking for a new job because of an unhealthy culture.

Every organization has a culture. In some companies the culture is implied, not expressly defined, and develops organically over time from the cumulative traits of the people the company hires. Sometimes businesses strategically craft a plan for what they want their brand and culture to be. Either way, it's impossible not to have a culture just as it's impossible not to have a brand. If someone doesn't care about their culture, brand, or reputation, not caring, in essence, becomes the organization's identifier.

WHEN THE VALUES OF THE CULTURE AND ACTUAL BEHAVIORS CLASH

Every organization has guiding principles that determine how it performs. These principles may be informal and develop organically, or judiciously crafted by senior leadership in the form of openly declared value statements. Sometimes observed behaviors inside the culture align with the proclaimed guiding principles, but, unfortunately, in the eyes of many employees they do not, resulting in one of the primary reasons employees leave.

The Society for Human Resource Management (SHRM) recently published findings from a series of surveys on the perceived condition of the workplace and its impact on working Americans that validated how widespread this discrepancy between employees' and leaders' perceptions of their culture exists. Almost all HR professionals (99%) agreed that they encouraged an open and transparent communication culture. Still, more than one in four working Americans (27%) did not think people leaders encouraged such transparency at all.

SHRM reported that 33% of working Americans indicated that their organization's culture makes it challenging to balance their work and home commitments, and three in ten employees (30%) said that their workplace culture made them irritable at home. The essential theme of these findings is that a company's culture will negatively impact the balance of an employee's 3-R scale by adding weight to the Requirements and decreasing the weight of the Rewards and Respect.

When employees see a misalignment of what a company says they value with the actual behaviors they observe, mistrust takes over and makes for a shaky ground on which an employee is to set their 3-R scale. For example, an organization may tout a value of social awareness and encourage employees to take company-paid time off to volunteer for their choice of meaningful causes. Yet, the approval process for getting the paid time off and finding coverage for their work while away may be so cumbersome and filled with endless red tape, they give up.

Another example where cultural misalignment occurs is when a company verbally places a high value on risk taking and encourages employees to think creatively. However, risk-taking behavior goes without positive recognition or incentives to encourage it; therefore, employees get the real message that the wiser choice is not to upset the apple cart. These types of organizational behaviors cause a foundational mismatch with employees' expectations upon joining a company with the reality of their experience, thus setting up additional shaky conditions on which employees' 3-R scales will sit.

Top performers are particularly aware of cultural misalignment. They do their homework researching an organization's digital presence, proclaimed causes, and demonstrated inclusiveness, and then check employee reviews to validate the claims. They look for culture authenticity with questions like, "If the organization supports giving back as part of the culture, is it ingrained daily or only during a special one-day event?"

Culture fosters a sense of identity and belonging—one of the basic human needs today's workers are seeking to fulfill. Whether it's the outcome of a purposeful, strategic initiative or left to develop on its own, ultimately healthy, or unhealthy, culture is always created by the highest level leader in control over the immediate group.

CULTURE INFILTRATES FROM THE TOP DOWN

While the CEO, president, or business owner may set the preliminary tone of a culture by structuring the company's values, each people leader under them will in turn create a mini culture within the team they are responsible for. The top in this case is the person directly leading the team. This is easily seen in how differently the mood and tone of each region, division, department, and team can feel within the same organization. The team culture under a narcissistic bully who manages by fear will feel quite different from the one led by a supportive servant leader.

While it is possible for pockets of healthy mini cultures led by remarkable people leaders to survive in unhealthy organizations, this situation is hardly ideal and definitely not sustainable as proven by more than one midlevel leader who has suffered through the need to buffer their team from toxicity at the top. Top performers will pass on joining a team with a leader who needs to spend energy on psychologically protecting them from higher leaders and instead will opt for authentic cultures with the following characteristics observable throughout all levels of leadership within the organization.

HEALTHY CULTURE CHARACTERISTICS

Respect: Everyone is treated with dignity and regarded for who they are as people.

Nurturing: Employees feel that their personal strengths are leveraged.

Appreciation: The focus is on what is right, not wrong.

Communication: There is an open exchange to freely contribute thoughts and ideas without fear of admonishment.

Access: Employees have access to information across all levels of the organization.

Learning: Everyone has opportunities for collaboration, coaching, and training.

Clarity: Employees fully understand the direction of the organization and the *why* behind any changes.

Accountability: Leaders and employees hold each other accountable for the integrity and acceptable behaviors they champion.

Encouragement: Despite setbacks, effort and initiative are recognized and rewarded.

Innovation: Employees are applauded for thinking creatively.

TAKE FIVE

1. Culture drives everything a company does or does not do.

2. It's impossible not to have a culture just as it's impossible not to have a brand. If someone doesn't care about their culture, brand, or reputation, not caring in essence becomes the organization's identifier.

3. Think of your company's culture as the base a 3-R scale will sit upon. A smooth and supportive base will uphold employee retention. An irregular and inconsistent base will result in employee turnover.

4. Culture fosters a sense of identity and belonging—one of the basic human needs today's workers are seeking to fulfill.

5. Whether it's the outcome of a purposeful, strategic initiative or left to develop on its own, ultimately healthy, or unhealthy, culture is always created by the highest level leader in control over the immediate group.

SURVIVAL TACTIC #1
HEALTHY CULTURE ASSESSMENT

Culture is an important foundation for a 3-R scale to be successfully set up and maintained. Complete the following assessment to determine the strengths and weaknesses of your current culture. Invite team members to complete as well and compare results.

(1)	(2)	(3)	(4)	(5)
Strongly agree	Agree	Neutral	Disagree	Strongly disagree

TRAIT	DESCRIPTION	SCORE 1-5
Respect	Everyone is treated with dignity and regarded for who they are as people.	
Nurturing	Employees feel that their personal strengths are leveraged.	
Appreciation	The focus is on what is right, not wrong.	
Communication	There is an open exchange to freely contribute thoughts and ideas without fear of admonishment.	
Access	Employees have access to information across all levels of the organization.	
Learning	Everyone has opportunities for collaboration, coaching, and training.	
Clarity	Employees fully understand the direction of the organization and the *why* behind any changes.	
Accountability	Leaders and employees hold each other accountable for the integrity and acceptable behaviors they champion.	
Encouragement	Despite setbacks, effort and initiative are recognized and rewarded.	
Innovation	Employees are applauded for thinking creatively.	

SURVIVAL TACTIC #2
TEAM MISSION STATEMENT

A team mission statement is a brief statement that describes a team's reason for existing. It helps to define the team culture and the way the team wants to be perceived. Team members work together to establish a common purpose and goal for their work together. The statement should also reflect the higher calling for the reason behind the work the team does.

How to create a team statement:

1. **What do we do?** In a few sentences, write down what your team does, what it delivers, or what it produces. If your team provides several different services or deliverables, choose the ones that account for 80% of the work. For example, *"Our team schedules patient follow-up visits."*

2. **Who are you doing this work for?** Clarify who your most important internal and external customers are. For example, are you scheduling patient follow-up visits for the home nurses or for the patients themselves? Be clear who you are partnering with.

3. **Why are we doing this work?** What is the ultimate outcome of the work you do? How is the final customer impacted? For example, *"Our team schedules patient follow-up visits so the nurses maximize the efficiency of their time in the field and the patients get the care they need in a timely fashion."*

OUR TEAM MISSION STATEMENT

What

_____

_____

_____

Who

_____

_____

_____

Why

_____

_____

_____

SURVIVAL TACTIC #3
TEAM ACCOUNTABILITY AGREEMENT

High performing teams have a team mission statement and hold each other accountable to fulfill it. The purpose of a Team Accountability Agreement is to come to a consensus on the rules of engagement to work together. All team members must be included in the creation of the Team Accountability Agreement. Review the agreement frequently and update as needed. Be sure to include it as part of the onboarding materials with new team members.

Here are examples of topics covered in a Team Accountability Agreement and questions to consider:

COMMUNICATION

- How will team members communicate with each other? What is the acceptable response time to messages?

- When are team meetings scheduled? What is the process if a team member is unable to attend? Who should attend the meetings? What is the expected behavior (virtually with camera on?) during the meetings? Will team meetings start and end on time? Who will monitor it?

DECISION-MAKING

- How will everyone have the opportunity to have a voice on team decisions?

- How will a final consensus be made by the team?

RESPONSIBILITY

- What is the process if unforeseen circumstances prevent a team member from completing a contingency project on time?

- What is the process if difficult or unclear responsibilities need to be voiced to other team members so that they can be clarified or redefined?

- How will concerns or issues that need resolution be processed?

LEADERSHIP

- Who is the primary facilitator for team meetings? Will it be rotated?

- Who is responsible for compiling the team agenda and directing the flow of the meeting?

CONSEQUENCES

- What is the process for not adhering to these team agreements? Who will enforce it?

TEAM ACCOUNTABILITY AGREEMENT

Team Name_____   Date_____

TOPIC	DESCRIPTION OF AGREEMENT

Team Signatures

14

GREAT FIRST TOUCHES MAKE FOR GREATER FIRST IMPRESSIONS

There isn't anything that will positively or negatively impact the initial balancing of a 3-R scale faster than the recruiting, interviewing, and onboarding experiences.

Initial encounters with a company are called first touches, and every one of them will make an indelible first impression. Think back to your own experiences. Do you recall a time when the company's online job application process was so cumbersome and frustrating you wanted to give up? And on top of that you never received an acknowledgment or follow up for your efforts?

Top performers, in particular, start auditioning a new employer upon every first touch, be it the recruiting process, emails, phone calls, texts, and follow-up procedures or lack thereof and will immediately begin slotting each experience into the company's culture plus or minus column. How about your first day on the new job? Was it one you fondly remember or a nightmare you'd prefer to forget? What about your onboarding experience? Were you sitting in front of a computer completing HR forms all day or was it a memorable time that was engaging, welcoming, and actively involving your leader?

These are all the many examples of the first touches with a business where the applicant's 3-R scale has already started to take shape and will set the tone of the true culture in a candidate's mind from the beginning. When it comes to culture, most top-performing candidates are not going to outwardly criticize the lackluster website, clumsiness of the application process, lack of an acknowledgment or thank-you, lag time to set up the interview, unprofessionalism of the office appearance, or negative interactions with the people involved—and it's extremely frustrating for a hiring manager to finally find the perfect candidate only to be turned down for what feels like a vague reason when in actuality the organization hit a third strike on the first touches.

VIRTUALLY RECRUITING

Research shows that it takes an interviewer about ninety-five seconds to make a first impression about the candidate. It would be safe to say it probably takes the candidate half that time to reach their first impression about the company. Companies must understand the importance candidates place on initial impressions in deciding whether they want to join an organization based on how they are treated during the recruiting process.

When the organization's best foot forward is supposedly on display, and a candidate has already racked up more negative touch points than positive ones (starting with bad directions to the company, inability to find a parking spot, and confusion about which door to go in), they will likely be thinking, "If this is the way they are treating me as a brand new candidate, what's it like to work here for a while?"

Review these five guidelines to see if your recruitment and interviewing first touches are making for greater first impressions:

- **Is the website updated and engaging?** Does the company website speak of action, excitement, edge, diversity, and purpose? Candidates checking out your website will expect nothing less. Companies are competing with every other media source to grab instant attention.

- **Is the online application process phone-friendly?** Candidates want instant access on demand. If the process is cumbersome and clunky, they won't spend time hassling with it. Make it easy and quick to complete on a smartphone. Start by asking a few skills assessment and screening questions. You can always get the résumé later.

- **Is your interview scheduling online?** Candidates are used to online scheduling options for just about any service they use today. They also want the flexibility of scheduling their own interview time. Avoid the potential of miscommunication and make manual attempts to set up times convenient for all.

- **Are the initial interviews offered virtually?** Even if the worksite is down the street, candidates want a first pass that is convenient, which typically means not in person. With all the access to meeting technology now, online everything is the expected norm of initial engagement.

- **Are candidates instantly informed and kept in the loop?** People are used to setting text alerts for anything they are expecting, which includes updates from a potential job connection. Top performers are overrecruited and want to know as soon as possible where they stand. A lag of information means no information to them, and they will quickly move on. The favored follow-up vehicle is text, not email, and definitely not phone calls.

IN-PERSON INTERVIEWS

The next potential first touch is an in-person interview where first impressions will also impact a 3-R scale. Candidates are interviewing a potential employer as much if not more than the employer is interviewing them. Applicants will pick up data points beginning the minute they drive into the parking lot. In-person first impressions are tremendously powerful in revealing a company's culture by the appearance of the office, the people milling about, and the tone of the environment. Is it fast paced? Laid back? Formal? Casual? Are people smiling and relaxed? Or is there an air of oppressive pressure?

It all matters to a candidate as they read the in-person culture. If they walk into a room where trash is overflowing, old coffee rings mar the tabletop, and half-filled water bottles are sitting on the windowsill next to three dead plants, it will not make the best impression. The Respect weight on their 3-R scale will also take a big hit if they are notified the night before that their next-day interview is canceled for no specific reason, or if they arrive on time but are left waiting in the reception area for twenty minutes while the interviewer is on the phone. Be mindful that the culture is on display as a result.

INTERVIEW FOR SKILL, FIT, AND 3-R SCALE BALANCE

Interview questions should determine a candidate's skill and culture fit as well as provide early indicators of the potential of a balanced 3-R scale. Once skill and culture fit are established, the focus of the future interviews should turn to getting an early sense of the weight the candidate will feel in meeting the direct and indirect Requirements of the job. Open-ended, 3-R–type questions will garner the most valuable information as opposed to closed ones.

Instead of asking, "Are you okay with an eight a.m. start time?" a more effective and realistic picture of the weight the candidate would assign to that Requirement would be determined by asking, "Tell me how an eight a.m. start time would impact your current schedule?" "What are the pros and cons of starting at that time?"

A hesitant reply of something like, "Would that be *every* day?" or "Well, I'm not a morning person, but I'll make it work," would provide a sense of the Requirements weight being much heavier than the candidate who says, "No problem. I've been getting up at five a.m. for an hour run every morning for the past ten years."

Another example of a 3-R scale question to determine their weighting of the Requirements would be something like, "As you think about the Requirements of the position, walk me through how you would structure your routine to ensure that meeting those Requirements would work for you."

In addition to getting an early awareness of the Requirements weights, uncovering how a candidate defines the Rewards and Respect they expect to get in return for doing the job is also important. If a candidate is moving forward for consideration, there will be an honest discussion of compensation, potential benefits packages, perks, and other items. In that discussion, a helpful 3-R question would include, "How do you define Rewards for doing a job?" and "What would you most value in return?"

Imagine how helpful for the leader when considering the candidate's potential 3-R scale balance upon hearing a reply of "money" as the most crucial Reward from one candidate, and "fast track promotions" from another, or "a sense of fulfillment and purpose" from still another.

At the end of the interviewing process there should be a strong sense of the candidate's skill, culture fit, skill capability, culture alignment, degree of the weight of the Requirements, and sense of what constitutes a Reward. The follow-up notes should include as much information about the 3-R scale balance as potential skill and culture fit.

Bottom line: businesses that are embracing the hiring changes in the new workplace are shifting from the old employer model of, "Here's what we offer," to the new approach of, "What do you need?" Culture matters when it comes to impacting a 3-R scale and the likelihood of ensuring its balance from the beginning.

First, as a major indicator of a company's culture, the interviewing process should ensure that the culture on paper matches the real culture as demonstrated by actual, observed behaviors the candidate personally experiences. Second, the interview questions asked of a candidate need to determine skill and capability, and the potential alignment of the weight of the Requirements, Rewards, and Respect going into the position. It is much easier for a leader to keep the scale balanced from the beginning as the honeymoon period wanes than trying to fix an already tilted scale sitting precariously on rocky ground.

ONBOARDING: THE GREAT UNVEILING OF CULTURE

A company's onboarding process is a direct gateway into its culture. Anything that happens during the onboarding process is sharply magnified in the new employee's eyes, both positively and negatively. A happy and satisfying onboarding experience plays a crucial role in setting up their 3-R scale for success, while anything less will result in damage control, and what people leader wants to be tackling that on a new hire's first days on the job?

Onboarding is when a business provides training and information to help familiarize new employees with their role and help them see how their position supports the company's overall purpose. According to a survey conducted by CareerBuilder and SilkRoad Technology, one in ten employees have left a company because of a poor onboarding experience, and 37% of employees said their manager did not play a critical role in their onboarding experience support.

Glassdoor noted that highly rated onboarding programs result in a retention improvement of 82%. A troubling statistic from Gallup found that only 12% of employees agree their organization does an effective job onboarding new hires. That means 88% do not believe organizations are successful at introducing new employees to their company.

Many businesses mistake employee orientation for onboarding. They are completely different. Orientation usually lasts a few hours to one day at most, with the goal being to complete all the necessary HR paperwork and other policy-related tasks.

Onboarding, on the other hand, is an extensive process that happens over a longer period of time. Depending on the type of organization, onboarding can last a few hours or up to a year. This is the time where new hires go to training, are gaining political savvy, and begin assimilating into the daily rhythms that make up the heartbeat of the organization. The kickoff event of an employee's onboarding experience begins with the all-important first day on the job. Day one is so important it can make or break a 3-R scale in a matter of minutes.

DAY ONE LASTS FOREVER

Do you recall the night before the first day of school? Despite the mournful musings that summer was officially over, for most of us it was filled with excitement, anticipation, a new book bag, and a fair amount of anxiety. How that first day turned out (who was in your homeroom, what lunch period you were assigned, which teacher you got for English, where your locker was, when you had study hall, right?) also set most of the tone for the entire year.

The same is true for an employee's first day on the job. The success of that first day is the responsibility of both the employee and their people leader. Employees need to make sure they set themselves up for success by arriving early or on time, looking the part, asking questions, being open to learning, and engaging with their coworkers. People leaders need to ensure that their employees leave at the end of their first day feeling enthusiastic, welcomed, and highly respected. On that first and only day, leaders have one shot to get it right.

JEAN AND JAYME'S FIRST-DAY RECAP

The first-day experience is especially critical to the early balance of a new hire's 3-R scale particularly in regard to adding weight to the Respect side.

If the day goes well, substantial Respect weight will be added instantly. If the day doesn't go well, Respect will quickly start to deplete as was the case with Jean. Take a minute and see what her day felt like.

It was one week ago today when Jean finally landed her dream job after rounds of interviews and jumping through all kinds of hoops. And today is her first day on the job. She arrives early to check in at reception only to learn they have no record of anyone starting that day. Twenty minutes later she is given a handwritten badge with her last name misspelled. She heads upstairs to the office where the administrative assistant greets her apologetically thinking her start day was next Monday, not today.

After another ten-minute wait, the inner door opens with a welcome from someone she recalls seeing in one of the interview panels. As she follows them down the hall to her workstation, she gets an apologetic heads-up from her escort who says, "It has been a bit crazy here lately, so the space isn't quite ready, but it definitely will be by tomorrow!"

She enters her assigned workstation to find an old copy machine, stacked boxes, a tilting chair (foreshadowing of her collapsing 3-R scale about now) and a desk that bears a cracked piece of edging and a dirty phone. But no time to fuss, her first team meeting starts in three minutes.

She enters the meeting room, is briefly introduced to her coworkers sitting around the table, and their leader quickly moves on to agenda item #1. The meeting concludes with a reminder that everyone is expected at the Beer-Brats-Bowling team fun event coming up Friday night (which happens to be the same time as her four-year-old's dance recital). Instead of a wonderful first day, in less than three hours, Jean is eyeing the exit door as she sits alone in the breakroom eating lunch with a 3-R scale that is already screaming "Tilt!"

Now live the first-day experience of Jayme. One week before her start date, she comes home to find a package on the front porch. Inside is a welcome card signed by every team member, a company swag bag, and the name and phone number of her First-Day Buddy with specific directions on where to check in and a detailed agenda of her first-day itinerary that includes a lunch out with her leader at a nearby restaurant.

As she arrives, she sees her buddy already in the lobby to greet her. The attendant at the counter introduces himself and promptly presents her with a professional-looking name badge and the correct spelling of her last name.

She is escorted to a spotless workstation to find a desk equipped with new supplies, a laptop set up with her log-in credentials, a map of the facilities, a menu for the on-site coffee shop, and a small basket of snacks with a note that says, "So Glad You Are Here."

Your first activity is a casual meet-and-greet with the team members over donuts and coffee in the breakroom. At the end of the day her leader makes a point to stop by and again expresses their delight to have her on board and asks how her first day went and if there is anything that could have made it better.

Jayme likely drove home with a 3-R scale so heavy with Respect she had trouble lifting it into the car.

Hopefully you get the idea by living out these two first-day scenarios. There's no going back to fix a bad first day.

NEXT FIRST TOUCH: NEW HIRE PROGRAM

Some of the reasons cited for a poor onboarding experience included that the new hire program was boring, mainly focused on processes and paperwork, too informal, haphazard, poorly run, thrown together, and inconsistent. Can you picture the Respect weight crumbling right off their 3-R scale? It's no wonder that, according to Digitate, a leading software provider, new hires who have a negative onboarding experience are twice as likely to look for a new opportunity in the future. This is exceptionally harmful to a company's bottom line knowing that the average US employer spends $4,000 and twenty-four days to hire a new worker.

There isn't any rocket science to making a new hire's training and onboarding time productive, meaningful, and engaging, nor is there any excuse for not doing so. Donuts are cheap and Respect is free. How a business makes a new hire feel will be an essential tool in adding weight to the Respect side of the scale. Helping them navigate the tough first weeks by streamlining processes and making sure procedures are easy, well-communicated, organized, and intentional will also go a long way to help lighten the initial weight of the Requirements.

Mentally go through your new hire's first day to experience it through their eyes, like spending a night in your own guest room. What does it feel like to arrive on your first day with no one knowing what's going on? How does it feel to be parked at some workstation and left there to plod through six HR mandatory training modules and dredge through a stack of three-ring binders stuffed with procedures? Make their beginning weeks as streamlined and easy to understand as possible.

The last thing any new hire wants in the beginning days on the job is unnecessary confusion. If the company's materials and tools are spread out in multiple locations, and if they are disorganized, sloppy, and confusing, that's a huge culture statement to the impressionable new hire. Think through the organization's entire recruiting and interviewing process, onboarding, and first day experience with a servant leadership mentality—one that puts the employee first.

Cultures that have strong onboarding experiences have many excellent traits in common. They create a feeling of safety, security, self-esteem, and belonging by eliminating confusion, ambiguity, anxiety, and unnecessary stress right up front. An excellent place to start may be interviewing the most recent employees who experienced the onboarding process and ask for their input and feedback. What better group to ask than the ones who just experienced it?

ONBOARDING REMOTELY

The on-site onboarding process takes conscious thought and detailed planning to execute successfully. This need is even more critical in a remote setting. There is no one close by to casually help fill in any unplanned stretches of downtime or to be readily available for a quick question on how to do something or to pop by the new hire's workstation for a quick check-in on how they're doing.

The remote onboarding process will also take longer because remote new hires are not in the office and privy to many activities that happen organically as part of their natural assimilation into the culture. There will be a critical need to strategically "structure spontaneity," as counterintuitive as that may sound. Creating a plan that will intently allow for the informal moments for the new hire to connect with others is vital in helping to mitigate the already existing potential for feeling disconnected and isolated.

There are several best practices among companies that have effective remote onboarding programs. They include the following:

- **Create a detailed onboarding plan.** Depending on the size and complexity of the business, it should cover a one- to two-week period.

- In the plan, **prearrange all meetings** (approximately two to four per day) to introduce critical individuals and essential processes.

- **Balance the meeting activities** with formal agendas and informal chats with no agenda, to get to know coworkers individually.

- **Make it fun.** Use engaging team photos and videos as part of the online welcome package. Have the new hire go on a virtual scavenger hunt or pick up clues from various people and places to solve a puzzle at the end.

- The **first day on the job is critical**, even more so virtually. Before their first day, send a welcome card and company swag gift. For the first-day lunch, have food delivered to the new hire's home and enjoy a virtual lunch together.

- **Assign a virtual buddy** for the first few days who is the new hire's primary go-to for all needs or questions, just like the on-site buddy. Ensure this buddy is readily available via instant messenger throughout the day.

- Make sure to **hold an end of first-day check-in** where you ask for feedback on how their first day went and preview the onboarding plans coming up.

- As part of the onboarding plan **provide a meaningful but smaller-scale project** to sink their teeth into right away. New hires want to make a couple of early home runs and create value as quickly as possible. What better way than by contributing to the work on a purposeful project?

- **Start holding 3-R conversations.** The onboarding time is critical to ensure their 3-R scale is in balance. Clarify how the new hire is weighting the Requirements needed to do the job, prioritizing the Rewards they most value, and determining whether the Respect being shown is in alignment with their definition.

The most central theme in successfully onboarding a new employee is to connect, communicate, and clarify. There is no risk in overly connecting, too much precise communicating, or wasting time spent (especially with a remote new hire) during the onboarding process. The basic human needs of emotional and psychological safety, belonging, and self-esteem are significantly increased when working remotely, requiring the onboarding process to be scaled up accordingly.

Everything must be done with an individualized and personal touch. Just sending a link that generically says "Onboarding Documents" and expecting them to filter through the 118 items to familiarize themselves is a sure-fire way to start dangerously light on the Respect side of the scale.

Recruiting, interviewing, and onboarding all make big statements about the organization's culture. And culture represents the foundation that each employee's 3-R scale will stand upon. If the culture is healthy, encouraging, and trusting, the 3-R scale starts out on a smooth, solid surface and has the best chance of staying that way.

TAKE FIVE

1. Interview questions should determine a candidate's skill and cultural fit as well as provide early indicators of the potential balance of a 3-R scale.

2. Research shows that it takes an interviewer about ninety-five seconds to make a first impression about the candidate. A candidate reaches their first impression of the company in half that time.

3. A company's onboarding process is a direct gateway into its culture. Anything that happens during the onboarding period is sharply magnified in the new employee's eyes, both positively and negatively.

4. People leaders need to ensure that their employees leave at the end of their first day feeling enthusiastic, welcomed, and highly respected. Leaders have one shot on that first and only day to get it right.

5. The on-site onboarding process takes conscious thought and detailed planning to execute successfully. This need is even more critical in a remote setting.

SURVIVAL TACTIC #1
3-R INTERVIEW QUESTIONS

Interview questions should determine a candidate's skill and cultural fit as well as provide early indicators of the potential of a balanced 3-R scale. Once skill and culture fit are established, the focus of the next interviews should turn to getting an early sense of the weight the candidate will feel in meeting the Requirements of the job. Check out these examples of 3-R questions to ask:

REQUIREMENTS

- Take a look at the major Requirements of this position (prepare a list of the direct Requirements). Which of these tasks are more favorable? Why? Which of these would be your less favorable? Why?

- In any working experience, what have you most enjoyed? Least enjoyed?

REWARDS

- Of the various items received in exchange for doing a job, such as compensation, benefits, and fulfillment, which are the most important for where you are in life right now?

- What other perks of the job would be most meaningful to you?

- What types of Rewards would be least meaningful?

- What was the best way you were acknowledged for doing an outstanding job? Why was it memorable?

- What do you most appreciate being recognized for at work?

RESPECT

- As you think about the previous leaders you have worked for, give some examples of what they did that made you feel the most respected.

- What did they do that made you feel the least respected?

- Trust is an important part of a successful working relationship. Give an example of when you felt a leader trusted you. Give an example of when you felt a leader did not trust you.

SURVIVAL TACTIC #2
FIRST-DAY CHECKLISTS

ON-SITE

√	PRIOR TO FIRST DAY
	Assign a buddy: Meets employee upon arrival and assists them the first week.
	Prepare first-day agenda: Set up meetings as needed.
	Make lunch plans: Make reservations or arrange to have food delivered.
	Prepare workstation: Clear and clean! Provide copy of first-day agenda, basic office supplies, water bottle, welcome sign, balloon.
	Prepare credentials: Arrange for ID card, badge, key fob, business cards.
	Prepare tech: Have equipment ready with software and log-ins.
	Mail welcome card to home: Have team members sign, include a company logo gift.
	Send welcome email: Include arrival details with map, address, parking instructions, lunch plans, list of nearby amenities, name of buddy who will meet them in the lobby.
	Prepare welcome event: Send invite to team for welcome coffee/donuts event.

√	FIRST DAY
	Lobby greeting: Have buddy meet employee in lobby to assist with check-in process and escort to workstation.
	Welcome event: Team members (include remotes) to gather for coffee and introductions.
	1:1 morning meeting with leader: Connect privately with employee early in the day.
	Lunch: Make it special. If delivered, invite other team members to join.
	1:1 end-of-day meeting with leader: Follow up on how the day went, ask for feedback on ways it could have been better, discuss itinerary for the rest of the week.

REMOTE

√	PRIOR TO FIRST DAY
	Assign a buddy: Virtually assists them the first week.
	Prepare first-day agenda: Set up meetings as needed.
	Make lunch plans: Arrange for lunch to be delivered to employee's home. Include lunch for remote workers and on-site team too. Set up virtual lunch time so all can eat together if logistics permit.
	Prepare welcome box: Send a package to employee's home that includes a welcome card, office supplies (or arrangements for ordering), company logo gift.
	Prepare tech: Get equipment ready for delivery with software and log-ins.
	Send welcome email: Include first-day itinerary, first-day log-in time, links to collaboration tools, IT contact. Copy buddy to assist with setup and questions during first week.
	Prepare welcome event: Arrange to deliver coffee and donuts to employee's home.
	Arrange for on-site meeting: If possible, set up an on-site visit during employee's first week.

√	FIRST DAY
	Welcome event: As possible, have all team members connect for coffee and introductions.
	1:1 morning meeting with leader: Connect privately with employee early in the day.
	Lunch: As possible, have all team members connect virtually for lunch.
	1:1 end-of-day meeting with leader: Follow up on how the day went, ask for feedback on ways it could have been better, discuss itinerary for the rest of the week.

15

THE POWER OF A 3-R LEADER

Don't be the leader you want to follow; be the leader your team wants to follow. Model the behavior you want. A good example is twice as powerful as great advice.

In Gallup's 2013 "State of the American Workplace" study, Gallup CEO Jim Clifton noted that the single biggest mistake businesses can make is to hire the wrong leaders. He is quoted as saying, "When you name the wrong person manager, nothing fixes that bad decision. Not compensation, not benefits—nothing."

And so much for the hope of creating a balanced 3-R scale.

Poor leadership has everything to do with negatively tilting a 3-R scale to the point that no possible size increase in the Rewards and Respect weights can counterbalance the Requirements of having to endure a bad leader. Gallup's report was released in 2013, and yet here we are years later still struggling with poor leadership. Why does it remain such an ongoing challenge?

To answer that question, let's start with an all too common way leaders get to be leaders. Almost every leader at one point began as an individual contributor. Their job was to just do their job. They were responsible from start to finish for completing a set of tasks that did not directly involve other people. An assembly worker was to turn out a daily quota of connected parts, a sales rep needed to meet a monthly goal of units sold, a teacher had to make sure the majority of students passed the upcoming standardized test. In all cases, the job involved a single worker and a set of tasks.

If an individual contributor happened to be notably successful at their job—the assembly worker's average was triple that of the expected quota, a sales rep consistently overachieved revenue gains by 150%, and every one of the teacher's students passed the standardized test—senior leadership took note and almost overnight the assembly line worker was now supervising a team of thirty other workers (mostly their former peers), the sales rep was promoted to district manager and was now coaching ten other sales reps to success, and the teacher was now working at the district office and supervising fifteen other teachers from multiple schools. And none of these new leaders received any formal training on how to lead people.

SHRM recently reported that over one in three working Americans (34%) indicated that their leader does not know how to lead a team. More than one in four managers (26%) said their workplace does not provide leadership training. In other words, these highly skilled workers went from hero to zero within a week.

DDI, a global leadership consulting firm, recently noted that 70% of frontline managers said they weren't expecting their promotion to leadership. While 20% were excited by the prospect of leadership, 17% only took the role because it seemed like the right next step. An additional 19% simply took it for the pay raise. Unfortunately, 18% of leaders also regretted taking the role, and another 41% have doubts about whether it was the right move. Being skilled at one's job certainly isn't a guarantee they will be effective at leading people.

New leaders reporting to bad leaders have an additional struggle to work through. Bad leadership simply promotes more bad leadership. If there is a fear of losing their job, people will tend to take on the traits and behaviors of the person they report to in the hopes they will be liked and kept in their favor. Sometimes it's a case of creating an emotional safety shield in which to survive a toxic culture. In any event it's a tragic occurrence that is still impacting the workplace today as all the latest research confirms that the primary reason people quit, especially top performers, is because of their leader.

Knowing their market value, top performers have little tolerance for inefficiencies, poor technology, inflexible processes, and definitely toxic leadership. There's also a case to be made that an employee doesn't leave a bad leader but, rather, leaves a bad organization. And there is truth to that. Organizations that tolerate bad leadership are endorsing bad behaviors, which perpetuates more of the same. Admirable leaders usually don't choose to stay in a toxic culture long enough to make a positive impact.

3-R LEADERS SERVE FIRST AND LEAD SECOND

In addition to attending formal leadership courses, gaining access to strong mentors, and modeling admirable people leaders, new people leaders can follow a few quick guidelines to help prepare for more effectively working with employees in today's new workplace.

Start by thinking about your preferred leadership style. Is it autocratic? Democratic? More situational? There are many different approaches to leadership. Some leaders prefer to focus on systems and processes as a way to efficiently get work done. Others take a more people-oriented approach. Both types are effective, and both are equally as important. Research shows that employees prefer leaders who can apply both styles as the circumstances call for it.

The pandemic, however, has resulted in a major shift from primarily getting work done through improved processes and efficiency gains, to a keen awareness of the need to care for the people doing the work, specifically their mental well-being and safety. As a result, those leaders who are naturally people oriented are more easily adapting to the new workplace. The transition for those leaders who come more from a process approach to a people approach can be made more easily by understanding what a people approach to leadership looks like and how to adopt it.

The best example of a people-orientation approach to getting work done is through a style called servant leadership. The term *servant leadership* was created by Robert K. Greenleaf in his 1971 essay, "Essentials of Servant Leadership." In practice, Southwest Airlines, under the guidance of founder Herb Kelleher, is frequently cited as the model servant leadership corporation resulting in a highly engaged, low-turnover workforce with thirty-five-plus consecutive years of profitability.

By encouraging their teams to work together, innovate, and share their opinions, servant leaders show their people that they are heard and appreciated. This approach has been proven in many studies to motivate teams to put their best effort forward and often results in higher quality work.

Servant-style leaders intuitively focus on employees as individuals and are likely already competent in addressing potential areas of dissatisfaction before they take root and result in turnover. These leaders are deploying a 3-R leadership approach by continually checking in with their team members to see if the weight of the job's Requirements has shifted and become heavier, and if the gains in the Rewards and Respect being given in return are keeping pace. They are serving the mental well-being needs of their people by asking 3-R questions that get at the root of what's needed for employees to feel balanced and satisfied in their positions. This universal style of leadership could not be more relevant in meeting employees' current cry to be treated as human beings.

THE LEADERSHIP STYLE OF CHOICE RIGHT NOW

Servant leadership focuses on the care and holistic well-being of people by relating to them as individuals first and employees second. Exceptionally skilled at making the individuals on their team feel like they matter, servant leaders demonstrate active listening and express appreciation, empathy, humility, trust, and caring. While these traits are certainly not mutually exclusive to servant leaders, the degree of consistency with which they demonstrate them is a differentiator.

Servant leaders also value their people for being the individuals they are. These leaders view their power as shared power and are not comfortable with self-promotion, preferring to attribute all success to the individuals they serve. They also score high in authenticity and transparency by the people they lead.

One of the tests a servant leader uses to measure their own leadership effectiveness is to ask if the people they are serving are growing as individuals. Are they becoming mentally wiser? More autonomous? Able to make effective decisions? How likely are they to become future servant leaders?

One of the loftiest goals a servant leader seeks to achieve is to see the day when their highly performing team no longer needs them. They achieve those desired results over time by balancing the right amount of empathy and understanding of their individuals' human side with the task and process drivers that must produce business results.

EMPATHY VERSUS SYMPATHY

Effective servant leadership incorporates behaviors that are positive as well as constructive. Just as with successful parenting, the right approach at the right time is key to the overall success of shaping the desired outcomes. This is important to think about as people leaders today are trying to balance the second most prevalent ask of employees (next to treat me like a human being): it is the expectation to be treated with empathy.

People leaders with a high degree of empathy can still empower their employees to meet business goals while at the same time express care for their sense of well-being. Empathy differs from sympathy in that it's not about taking pity or just feeling sorry for someone. Employees want to have a sense that their leader understands what it's like to be in their situation. They want their leader to listen to their concerns, see the world from their perspective, and relate to their feelings.

If an employee is expressing concerns about meeting multiple deadlines with the added pressure of overseeing the virtual schooling of three children along with caring for an elderly family member, a leader who responds with, "I'm so sorry to hear that, what are you going to do to make sure you don't miss the project deadline?" is anything but empathetic and one that would likely have the employee mentally screaming, "What am I going to *do*? Probably quit!"

As opposed to another leader listening to the same employee's concerns who replies with, "That's a lot to balance and I can see it's a bit overwhelming to say the least. So, let's not focus on everything we can't control. Instead, let's work together to prioritize what you can manage right now and take one step at a time to make that happen." This type of messaging will go a long way in communicating a sincere sense of care and empathy.

Like most approaches to anything, too much of something can be counterproductive. A new term surfacing in the workplace among people leaders is *empathy fatigue*. It can be emotionally draining to consistently balance expressing the right amount of empathy with the need to ensure that business results are still achieved. Some leaders feel that it is hard for them to consistently demonstrate empathy in the workplace for fear of being less respected, and others find that being empathetic holds an inherent risk of not getting their own needs met. Neither approach is beneficial.

The leaders who do the best job of balancing empathy with meeting business results have two important traits in common:

- They always treat people respectfully.

- They maintain accountability.

EMPATHY MINUS ACCOUNTABILITY: A BAD EQUATION

Empathy is not the removal of the goal; it's consideration for how the goal is achieved. The goal doesn't go away. An employee may have an onset of personal issues that are preventing them from getting to work on time. The forgiveness of breaching a policy on rare occasions is empathy. Helping the employee to set a course of action to prevent their tardiness, while still holding them accountable to meet the expectation of being on time, is empathy. Letting the employee continue to arrive late almost every morning because of personal challenges, however, is not empathy. It's enablement. A leader who enables employees not only harms the employee but the leader's reputation and respectability among other team members as well.

Effective coaching encourages employees to take ownership of working out their own solutions and counsels them with an understanding that even though their personal circumstances are indeed unsettling and challenging, adding work performance issues on top of them is not going to be in their best interest.

Leaders who effectively balance empathy with productivity always seek to understand before being understood. They remain more curious than judgmental. They are curious about their own reactions and what is causing frustrations with an employee and want to better understand the source of their employee's issue to seek ways to coach and guide them through it but without removing accountability for doing their job.

You can't force someone to become accountable; you can only assign them responsibility, which is different from their taking ownership. By not holding someone accountable for meeting their responsibility is where too much empathy can result in enablement and perceived favoritism.

THE UNIQUE CARE AND SERVING OF TOP PERFORMERS

Another primary aspect of servant leaders is the care and attention they give to ensure that equal time is paid to each of their people, particularly top performers. It's not about treating them with favoritism, it's more about remembering that they are human beings with the same needs as the others on the team and giving them their due attention accordingly. Top performers are the ones who most readily stand out on a team and yet risk being the most hidden from their leader at the same time.

The common mistake some people leaders make with a top performer is assumption. Because they are typically self-starters, need little if any coaching to succeed at their work, and rarely have any issues or drama to resolve, top performers can too easily be put on autopilot with the assumption that everything is fine, and no news is good news. When schedules are crunched, it can be too easy to skip a 1:1 meeting with a top performer to focus on administrative tasks or redo the unsatisfactory work of a low performer.

As people first, top performers are no different in their basic needs from other team members, and wise servant leaders make sure they are consistently receiving the attention needed.

WHY EMPLOYEES WANT A SERVANT LEADER

Servant leadership has many advantages over other leadership styles in this current environment because of the emphasis it places on the human aspects of work and how it aligns with employees' needs, as spoken in their own words:

- *Get to know me as a real person.* How much do you know about the human side of me? Get to know me. Ask me about my dreams and aspirations. Favorite fast-food place, or snack. Ask me to share about my hobbies. Let me know that you are interested in hearing my story. Do you know who the most important players are in my life? How about what I do well and not so well?

- *Do 20% of the talking.* When we meet, please do more listening and less telling. Ask thought-provoking open-ended questions where I have to think about the answers and then listen like you intently mean it. Confirm what I said, play back what you heard, and please look me in the eye. Keep the distractions away, put the device down. I want to feel like I am the most important person at that moment, the one you want to keep at all costs.

- *Give me no doubt that you have my back.* Please be generous with your support. If I fall, I want to know you will be the first one there to pick me up. If I happen to have a meltdown, I need to know you'll be there on the spot with the mop, bucket, and no judgment.

- *De-escalate, don't dump.* We all want to care for our mental well-being and for each other. Please don't ratchet up my stress intensity by sharing your own frustrations and uncertainties with me. It's unsettling. Create a sense of calm rather than anxiety even when you're not all that sure about some of the outcomes yourself.

- *Be humble and vulnerable.* It's okay to embrace your humanness and authenticity. Saying "I don't know" is fair. Actions are more powerful than words. Model the actions you want me to follow. The behavior I see you do is the behavior I will trust to be more real.

Adopting a servant leadership style is a major step at becoming a successful leader of people. And there are many more attributes to aim for in the attempt to finally turn around the cycle of perpetuating bad leadership because of poor selection processes or lack of training or for allowing toxic cultures to support it.

The following quick guide will hopefully create a new set of standards for promoting individual contributors to leadership roles, as well as empower leaders who need a positive role model (even if it is on paper). These points will not only put you in the mindset where employees currently need you to be as their current leader, it will also prepare you to naturally embrace the concept of helping your top performers talk about the balance of their 3-R scale and how you can work together to ensure they feel fulfilled and engaged and are productively meeting business goals.

3-R LEADER QUICK LIST

- **Adopt a servant-style leadership approach.** It's not about you, it's about the people you are leading. Be humble, vulnerable, human, and smart.

- **Know your people as individuals.** Everyone is unique. The better you know your team as human beings, the better you can lead each one of them.

- **Hold 3-R conversations often.** Ask 3-R questions that will uncover how each person is weighting the Requirements they are being asked to meet with the balance of the Rewards and Respect they are getting in return. Check in regularly to adjust the weights as needed.

- **Showcase purpose and fulfillment.** Keep the higher calling, the reason the business exists, front and center. Remind people often of how they are contributing to it with their individual work.

- **Encourage risk and innovation.** Actively listen to everybody and every idea. No judgment. Motivate others to get creative.

- **Model and reward the behaviors you want.** If you want integrity, model it. If you want honesty, be honest. If you want respect, be respectful. Whatever you do, you will get in return. The team pays attention to your actions, regardless of your words.

- **Create calm not chaos.** Poor communication, unnecessary meetings, dropping your own drama, and fanning burnout flames are mega sources of stress for the team. Aim to be a source of quiet purpose and confidence, despite the flurry of feet paddling just below the surface.

- **Come from gratitude.** Celebrate something positive every day. Point it out to the team and recognize them for it. Share the credit and realize you could have never achieved the results on your own. Look for what is going right and build on it.

- **Speak the truth.** It's not easy for *leaders* to *speak* their mind, especially when the popular opinion is the opposite. But a courageous *leader* speaks *truth*, at all times.

- **Delegate and empower.** Find the delicate balance of delegating without micromanaging. Determine the skill and will level of any specific task for an employee and balance the right amount of directive behavior and the need for hands off as the circumstances dictate.

The combination of these characteristics results in a truly appreciated and highly respected leader of people. Their team doesn't just admire them; they want to do whatever it takes to please them out of a return of respect for what they do for them. There is no better way to lead, get results, or counterbalance an employee's decision to stay when the Requirements weight may be unduly hefty and the Rewards weight questionably light. Where possible, employees will stay longer in a situation where they are valued, respected, and appreciated.

TAKE FIVE

1. The servant leadership style most aligns with employees' current needs of wanting to be treated like human beings and with empathy. This approach focuses on the care and holistic well-being of people by relating to them as individuals first and employees second.

2. The leaders who do the best job of balancing empathy with meeting business results have two important traits in common: (1) They always treat people respectfully; and (2) They maintain accountability.

3. Servant leaders ensure that equal time is paid to each of their people, particularly top performers. It's not about treating them with favoritism; it's more about remembering that they are human beings with the same needs as the others on the team and giving them their due attention accordingly.

4. When schedules are crunched, it can be too easy to skip a 1:1 meeting with a top performer to focus on administrative tasks or redo the unsatisfactory work of a low performer.

5. Be humble and vulnerable. It's okay to embrace your humanness and authenticity. Saying "I don't know" is fair. Actions are more powerful than words. Model the actions you want your team members to follow.

SURVIVAL TACTIC
3-R LEADER INVENTORY

3-R LEADER TRAIT	WHAT I'M DOING WELL	HOW I CAN GROW
Be a strong servant leader.		
Know every team member as an individual.		
Hold ongoing 3-R conversations with all employees, starting with top performers.		
Showcase purpose and fulfillment behind the work being done.		
Encourage risk and innovation.		
Model and reward the behaviors you want.		
Create calm not chaos.		
Come from gratitude.		
Speak the truth.		
Delegate and empower.		

16

ON-SITE, REMOTES, AND HYBRIDS, OH MY!

Never have so many people been connected to so many others,
and yet more people than ever are suffering from loneliness.

The merging onset of globalization, decentralization, and technology along with the movement of the flattening of formal reporting hierarchies to self-governing work teams and 24/7 access to information and people anytime, anywhere have completely redefined the norms of employer-employee engagement. The only thing we know for certain about the future of flexible working options is that it's in flux for every organization as they continue to work through the options.

Three work models have emerged since the pandemic: completely remote working from home, completely working on-site, or a hybrid, combining on-site days with remote time during any given week. Depending on the organization, there is hesitancy about solidifying exactly what their return-to-work policies will require. Company deadlines for calling people back into the office keep getting pushed back. Concerns about instilling polices that may worsen the "I quit" movement tend to ebb and flow with the latest mandates of the moment. The feedback on the overall success of flexible work options ranges widely.

Productivity is up, productivity is down. Leaders love it. Leaders hate it. Employees are evenly split on preferences for working on-site, working from home, or a combination of the two. You name it, you can build a case for it. For the near term it's at least safe to say providing flexible work options in some capacity is here to stay, as employees will continue to insist on having choices in industries where that is possible.

What we also know is that it takes a different skill set to lead remote or hybrid workers. People leaders will need to meet many new challenges to engage and keep them, not to mention create and maintain an inclusive and collaborative team culture in the process.

New workplace paradigms are in flux and being refined at this moment. Employers are trying to figure out how to make it all work while HR teams are in overdrive trying to balance the execution of needed business processes with a new emphasis on employee expectations. For organizations and people leaders managing teams within this mix and myriad of working environments, special considerations are needed to balance an employee's 3-R scale. One truth that will always remain the same is that people are still *people,* first—no matter the working environment. However, the activities to care for that concept will need to be shifted accordingly.

NOT EVERYONE IS WIRED TO WORK REMOTELY

Whether remote working is part of an employee's hybrid model, or 100% of their environment, without a doubt the remote world is here to stay because of all the freedoms it has unleashed. It's Pandora's box in a sense and there is no going back. With all the technical advantages and benefits the online world provides like working across multiple time zones, instant access to information 24/7, ability to work anytime and from anywhere, availability of a global stage to express opinions, and knowledge sharing, it has not arrived without its challenges for many employees. Some thrive, some manage, and others are imploding.

Recent studies looking at remote workers found that those who are most likely to succeed have a proclivity toward agreeableness; they take most events and outcomes in stride, focus on the positive, and are considered easy going. Those who are struggling are the ones who are highly alert to their surroundings and deal with an underlying turmoil of continual anxiety and pressure, which is only made worse working in an environment where the human factor is absent.

Never have so many people been connected to so many other people, yet more people than ever are suffering from loneliness. Before the onset of the digital world, relationships with friends, partners, leaders, and coworkers happened more organically and developed naturally over time. The primary way people communicated was through body language and facial expressions.

Living on a digital platform is drastically changing all that. The natural building of relationships and ensuing fellowship with others is displaced with the need to schedule spontaneous interactions and second-guess the meaning of intended words in an instant message. We've resorted to getting to know someone through nothing more than a computer screen, email signature, or the now obsolete phone call.

Despite one's feelings about working remotely, almost everyone has been frustrated by its confines. People leaders need to be aware of these issues as any one of them, at any time, can quickly start piling more weight to the Requirements side on an employee's 3-R scale.

WORKING FROM HOME: EMPLOYEES' CONCERNS

- **Technology:** Intermittent Wi-Fi connections, malfunctioning equipment, and lack of on-site help are always in the back of the minds of remote workers, especially the night before a big presentation. Not being on-site for the ability to call IT, or at least to be in the immediate cue for resolution, is an ongoing concern. (One tip for a trouble-free connection is to hard wire the computer with a Cat-5 cable directly into the router.)

- **Distractions:** For the naturally unorganized or undisciplined, distractions of any sort will wreak havoc on their productivity. People in this category are going to need help creating and sticking to a strict schedule.

- **Isolation:** With no one to run down the hall and see or connect for a quick breakroom chat, loneliness is one of the primary concerns reported among almost all remote workers. Work is social time for many as well, so the lack of the human connection starts to weigh heavily after a time. Leaders are trying a combination of ideas like sporadically setting up virtual team watercooler time with no agenda other than to hang out a bit and chat.

- **Diminished collaboration:** A lack of face-to-face time makes team building challenging and hinders natural collaboration. Little if any relationship collateral can be built upon and allowed to grow naturally. Messaging each other isn't a replacement for human interaction. It is essential for businesses with remote workers to invest in a high-quality collaboration software.

- **Perception of not working:** Remote workers are reporting that they are working even harder from home to overcome any stigma of not carrying their load. This aligns with pressure they report feeling from always having to be on and compelled to immediately respond to messages on personal time as well as work time.

- **Lack of work-life balance:** When business and personal life blur, everything becomes "bursonal," and remote workers report they are definitely living in a bursonal world. Working from home creates a never-ending opportunity to open the laptop for just five minutes, which too many times turns into an hour.

- **Out of sight, out of mind, and passed over:** Because of their lack of office visibility, many remote workers have a fear of becoming out of sight, out of mind, and passed over for promotions as a result. Remote workers are at risk of being left out of the impromptu decision-making moments leaders may make about their promotability. Demonstrating three-dimensional advanced leadership skills like conflict resolution, emotional intelligence, and relationship building in the moment can be more challenging with only an online presence.

MINIMIZING REMOTE WORKER BURNOUT

- **Stop asking, "How's it going?" "How are you doing?" or "What do you need from me?"** These generic questions will solicit the same generic answers as, "fine," "okay," and "not much." Go deeper and get to know how remote-strong each of your workers is feeling and where they specifically need you to lighten the weight of the Requirements or balance it with additional Rewards and Respect. Start asking 3-R questions like, "Tell me how you are feeling about your Requirements weight this past week. What changed, if anything, that made it heavier? Or made it lighter? Are the Rewards and Respect weights balancing any changes in the Requirements? If there's an imbalance, where is it and what needs attention?"

- **Listen to what's *not* being said.** Pay attention to how your remote employees express themselves in between what they are actually saying. Listen for their tone of voice and energy level. While on camera take note of posture, body language, declining change in appearance. Give your remote employees your undivided and frequent attention. Let them vent, confide, and feel emotionally safe enough to say they feel disconnected and why.

- **Recognize and reward.** After asking their preference in how to be recognized, go out of your way to look for what they are doing right and reward accordingly. Sometimes just a simple thank-you for the slightest of actions can go a long way in providing meaningful attention when you're remote and alone.

- **Respect personal boundaries.** Model the ability to compartmentalize work and personal life by leading with a healthy respect for boundaries. Avoid sending any messages outside of work hours and ask the team members to do the same with each other. If you choose to work whenever convenient and use Sundays as your communication catch-up time, use the delay-send option, or craft your messages and wait until the next workday to post. People will look at your 1:00 a.m. time stamp and think, "Really?" Oh, and that caveat of "sorry to bother you on the weekend, please don't feel you have to respond until Monday" note? It is not helpful. The damage is done, the pressure is on. Even if your employee doesn't reply as requested, they now have to think about it or feel compelled to check messages on personal time because their leader has a habit of sending them then.

- **Pay attention to time and mental breaks.** If you are a global business, try to switch up meeting times so that no one group always gets the convenient 10:00 a.m. hour and someone else gets stuck with the 10:00 p.m. slot. Encourage remote team members to schedule time away from their workstations. Model the importance of taking mental breaks to keep the brain sharp.

- **Encourage and reward time off.** In the past year, 11% of remote employees say they've taken a day off specifically to get caught up on work. Fifteen percent of remote workers didn't take any days off in the last year, and almost half (46%) took only a week or less off. Make sure PTO policies are user friendly and clear. Model the way by ensuring you are taking time off as well. And make it real time off by modeling that it's acceptable to drop out and disconnect by setting your online presence to "away" and that you will answer messages upon your return.

- **Combat loneliness.** Keep the focus on the team's mission and why everyone is there each day. Populate the calendar every few days to hold impromptu chat sessions that have no agenda and no pressure to attend—just an open space for team members to congregate organically for a few minutes. Get socially creative. Host a monthly event like a Teammate Scavenger Hunt or People Bingo to encourage team connections.

Bottom line: the best way to assess the risk factors for burnout is to directly seek feedback from your employees both remotely and on-site. Keep the communication channels open with your people and use those channels often. Keep talking it out. Be relatable. It's okay to admit that there's a lot going on for everyone right now and we are all on the same team trying to figure it out together. In the midst of so much change fatigue and ambiguity, you want to be the leader who aims to calm.

THE BIGGEST REMOTE CHALLENGE: BUILDING TRUST

Making the transition from leading a team in a single location where all or some of the members are now working remotely or in a hybrid model presents a steep learning curve at best in normal times. Add a global pandemic and that upward curve just became Mt. Everest. When people undergo a radical change, psychological safety and the ability to trust can take a big hit.

Trust is foundational to any relationship, and without it in the workplace, the result is miscommunication, multiple meetings to clear the air, and pervasive blame and conflict.

Remote working has stripped away one of the basic tendencies of human nature: to trust only in what we can see. Historically, organizations have been reluctant to provide remote working options because an employee's performance was primarily based on physical observations like their presence in the office or hours punched on a time clock. The shift to managing remote employees has been a challenging one for some leaders, especially those with a high need for control. Many people leaders liken an employee's remote productivity with that of being physically seen working in person and making the mistake of assuming that hours worked correlate to the quality of output. Hours are never a fair indicator for remote efforts.

It wasn't until there was no other choice but to send employees home to work that organizations had to embrace it, and many people leaders are still seeking to find a balance between the tendency to micromanage and trust.

There are two areas of focus for building trust. First, establishing a trusting relationship with every individual member on the team is key. This is a perfect opportunity for a 3-R conversation especially as it relates to Respect. Asking each person to define what trust looks like for them and how it can best be manifested between the two of you will help to bring clarity to the actions and behaviors you will want to demonstrate with them as their leader and those you will want to avoid.

Second, by modeling trusting behaviors you will help to instill trust among the team members as well. The level of collaboration and teamwork required for high performance teams depends on trust and mutual respect with everyone working together. Welcome and encourage diverse ideas and experiences. Those differences are what make the team stronger. Hold a 3-R team meeting around what trust looks like for each other. Sharing those insights together can help to create an appreciation of respectful behaviors needed within the team. By using a 3-R approach for building trust, you are acquiring five of the most important healthy culture characteristics: respect, nurturing, appreciation, communication, and access to information.

A trusting people leader and safe organizational culture are nonnegotiable for any employee looking to join an organization today. Make trust your default outlook. Decide that you are going to first come from trust, until someone makes it clear they cannot be trusted. This is exceptionally important when it comes to employees working remotely. People want to be trusted to get their work done. Ensure your communication and directions leave no margin for what's expected.

SUCCESSFUL REMOTE GUIDELINES FOR PEOPLE LEADERS

- **Provide transparency, visibility, and accessibility.** Be as visible and as forthcoming as possible. Set up common share sites where notes, updates, and information the team can benefit from are readily available. Proactively address any elephants in the room. Don't ignore or bury issues that need to be dealt with. Maintain consistency in remote policies like camera connections required as part of your meeting protocol. Respond promptly to all messages.

- **Present the why.** Share your vision. Keep purpose and fulfillment of the bigger picture a regular part of your leadership tool kit. Employees who understand the why and the higher calling for reasons behind the work they do are more motivated and want to intrinsically achieve. Look for ways to help employees connect their activities to the company's bottom line. For each major project, have team members describe the benefits and financial impact of their work and how it will ultimately benefit the organization's goals.

- **Seek continual growth.** Even the best teams improve from feedback and learning from their mistakes. Model a growth mindset by first asking for feedback on ways you can get better as the leader. Keep the request for feedback specific. Instead of asking, "How am I doing as your leader?" (to which you'll more than likely hear "fine" even from those who don't think it's fine), make the request with something such as, "I'd like your feedback on how I explained the changes in the new reporting format at our team meeting yesterday. I'm not certain I was as clear on the reasons for the changes as I could have been. Any suggestions for what I could have done differently?" Focus on continuous learning and invest time in your team members' growth.

- **Continuously reassess.** The attainment of perfect processes and relationships will never remain that way, and people leaders who foster a mentally safe environment and a culture of trust will allow their teams to weigh in on ideas to pursue continuous improvement. Listen actively, repeat what you're hearing as a way to check for understanding. And most importantly act on their ideas, as feasible. Even the smallest change that the team sees implemented as a result of their feedback will result in stronger bonds of trust.

- **Build community.** Always come from a people are *people*, first approach and build a strong community of human beings. As possible with time zones, hold a weekly huddle as part of the team rituals where everyone has a few minutes to talk about anything that's on their mind. Make the discussion not about work. Create virtual spaces where people have the freedom to get to know each other through the screen. Make it fun, with a trivia question of the week, or share a photo that best described the weekend. A sense of familiarity can help to build a sense of collaboration and community among the team.

A TALE OF TWO CULTURES

Building a strong, cohesive culture is critical in providing an environment where employees can maintain a balanced 3-R scale and continue to thrive. Building that culture is challenging enough when everyone is in one office. To attempt to do so with employees in widespread locations with the likelihood of never meeting each other in person is daunting at best. A remote culture is a subculture within the team culture. The biggest challenge for people leaders is the ability to break down the walls of the on-site culture and the remote culture in order to blend the two.

Just as office-based employees need a sense of a higher calling as to why they come into work every day, remote employees need the visibility of that higher purpose amplified even more so to avoid getting lost in their isolating day-to-day workload. A remote employee also has an inherent risk of a tilted 3-R scale with heavy Requirements because of this potential lack of purpose. They can easily fall into the claim of "I'm laying bricks" instead of "I'm erecting a magnificent cathedral." Building a solid culture must be intentional. Just as with an on-site culture, a remote culture will take on a life of its own if left unattended.

For starters, make sure your team culture is not hampered by poor technology from within the organization. Businesses need to take a hard look at the ease with which remote workers can access company sites, collaborate with coworkers, and navigate areas outside their departments. In addition, what is the availability and quality of tech support needed? Are any of these processes adding unnecessary weight to the Requirements side of the employee's scale?

In addition to building trust, communication is a foundational block of a cohesive culture. Communication must be frequent, purposeful, and transparent, especially between a people leader and their direct report. It's the lifeline to feelings of safety, belonging, self-esteem, and purpose when leading remote employees. Just because people are remote, their basic human needs don't go away. It's also a two-way street. Employees have a tremendous responsibility to keep their leaders informed and aware of their work.

As a final point, a strong remote culture has clearly defined rules of engagement that guide employees' expectations in a remote workplace, such as these:

- Is there a required log-on time?

- Outside of meeting attendance, are employees expected to be available as needed?

- Do all employees need to be responsive to coworkers within twenty-four hours across multiple time zones?

- How are meeting times cared for across time zones?

- Is there a stipend for home office setup? If so, are the purchasing guidelines clear?

- Will remote employees be required to attend in-person meetings or come to the office on certain days or for additional events?

- Is "video on" always a requirement when leaders and employees are in virtual meetings?

- What is the collective feedback mechanism for remote employees to share their experience, best practices, and any suggestions for improvements?

The more details and clarity built into a remote culture, the fewer potential issues for employees to misinterpret what will be expected of them. The bottom line: most employees want to show up and do their best work within an environment that feels accepting, rewarding, and supportive. When that environment is remote, it takes concentrated effort and extra mindfulness to create a culture that will result in those desired outcomes.

BEWARE OF PROXIMITY BIAS

Employees who express a fear of being out of sight and out of mind have a rational reason for doing so. New research is showing that people leaders with remote team members may show an unconscious favorability toward those team members they see in the office and interact with face-to-face on a frequent basis. The term is *proximity bias* or *face time bias* and is one of the leading reasons remote workers express a lack of appreciation and recognition from their leader.

We all have biases when it comes to interacting with people. When presented the opportunities to engage with others in person, it is natural to want to align with those we seem the most comfortable around. Biases are usually unconscious, and their effects are not consistently recognized. Because of a stronger sense of familiarity, people leaders falling prey to proximity bias will tend to deem those employees as better workers and thus more highly valued than their remote counterparts.

Leaders will need to be extra diligent to ensure they are not unconsciously favoring those they see over those they physically don't. So much of the natural, one-off casual conversations that take place on-site can easily fuel this type of bias and create a halo effect, resulting in a false sense of viewing that person more favorably, built on no more than familiarity.

Employees close to their leaders tend to get the best projects with the highest organizational visibility, often based on the leader's inflated value of the employee's skill sets. This bias can taint even the most objective review of information unfairly. A leader can review the same presentation submitted by two employees and give high marks to the one with the favorable bias and low marks to the one outside the favorability circle.

The reverse of this principle also is observed, resulting in leadership looking the other way or making excuses for a poor performer who has won favor because of physical proximity while not fairly assessing the real value offered by those the leader simply has less contact with.

If the issue of proximity bias goes unchecked, the remote employee's 3-R scale will be negatively impacted due to a lack of Respect. This sustained preferential behavior as observed by remote employees sitting outside the proximity bias circle has the potential for creating a feeling of "no matter how hard I work, I still don't get the same recognition."

As a result, this outlook will sharply decrease the Respect weight on their decision scale and at the same time increase their Requirements weight as they burn out trying to do three times the amount of work in hopes of getting one-fourth the recognition. This perceived favoritism will also impact productivity and motivation, potentially harboring an employee's mindset of doing no more than what's needed to stay out of trouble. It's the employee's way of self-calibrating their 3-R scale to survive the job. The thought being, "Since I need to keep this job at least for the time being, I'll take it upon myself to decrease the Requirements, to balance with the little Respect I'm getting in return."

STEPS TO PREVENT PROXIMITY BIAS

- **Watch out for it.** Now that you have a sense of what proximity bias is, watch for it in yourself and among team members. Is the amount of time you spend interacting with each team member equal? If an office-based team member is on a virtual team meeting, do you tend to hold more frequent and longer conversations with that person? The remote employees are definitely picking up on that.

- **Create and expect equal interaction time for all.** Do not hold separate meetings for the on-site group and the remote group. This is a guaranteed way to build two separate and strongly divisive cultures. The entire team, if possible, should be included regardless of their working environment. Send the meeting agenda out in advance and ask each team member to prepare their thoughts and contribute to the discussion. When holding a virtual meeting, monitor and enforce equal participation. Make a list of the attendees' names and use checkmarks to keep track of equally including everyone in the discussions and how much each one is talking.

  Make a point to use everyone's name and find something positive to call out about each one. It may be as simple as, "DeTrae brings up a meaningful point, let's build on that." When you ask for feedback on a particular topic, go around the gallery and call on each person individually to get their pros and cons.

Finally, watch for virtual cliques. Because of proximity bias, on-site members who see each other often may be taking a lot of team-meeting virtual time to engage with each other at the expense of remote employees watching it in the background.

HYBRIDS: HUH?

Companies are using the nebulous term *hybrid* in so many ways these days that even *Merriam-Webster* is struggling to come up with an applicable workplace definition, especially when you add the word *flexible* to it. Hybrid can mean anything from going into the office a few days a week but maybe not all weeks, or working in the office a few hours a day, but not the same hours and not on every day, and maybe working from home one whole week, but not all weeks, when on different days half the time could be in the office, but not always the same half of the same day—well, you get the picture why over 30% of employees feel there is a lack of clarity around when to work in the office, when to work from home, and what type of work should be done in either place. That's a hybrid—with flexibility.

The first step an organization must take is to clearly define their hybrid vision and then arrange the workplace norms around that vision so that it's clear, communicated, and stabilized. Start the process by asking these questions:

- What exactly does hybrid mean in your organization?

- What does it look like on your team?

- What does it look like for each role?

- Is it different for each person? Is it equitable?

- What are the expectations for working in the office?

- What are the guidelines for holding a virtual meeting on-site where office workers are?

- How will collaboration be maintained among all team members regardless of work location?

- Will all people be required to be in the office at some time?

- Will employees have an assigned on-site workstation? Hot desk?

- Is this a one-size-fits-all hybrid approach?

- Have you included the input and feedback from employees who will be impacted?

Keep asking and drilling down into these questions to create as much clarity around your hybrid guidelines as possible to address the most common concerns employees are expressing about working in a hybrid environment:

- Lack of clear expectations of when and how often to go into the office and for what reasons

- Lack of consistency in the execution of hybrid guidelines and protocols

- Lack of equal opportunities for those who are working in a hybrid environment

- Having no input on the design and outcomes of the company's hybrid polices

REQUIREMENTS HIDING IN A REMOTE WORLD

Depending on the individual, working remotely can either impact an employee's 3-R scale balance positively or negatively. Working remotely comes with an additional set of challenges that may add hidden weight to the Requirements side of an employee's balance scale. If leaders are not aware of them and on the lookout, unevenness can quickly creep up on an employee's 3-R scale and create enough of an imbalance to cause them to quit when, all along, an astute leader could have managed it.

Employee engagement is more at risk digitally than on-site, not only because of the potential for isolation but also due to the high level of outside distractions. Employees working in a remote world are 2.54 times more likely to experiences digital distractions than on-site employees. These include everything from technological disruptions like unstable Wi-Fi and inadequate home office equipment to daily life interrupters like doorbells, pets, children, service providers, spilled cereal, and off-balance washing machines. Any of these interruptions break concentration and the cognitive flow needed to resume the task.

Multiple studies confirm that distractions derail the brain's ability to refocus, and it can take up to twenty-five minutes to regain the concentration needed to get back to the task. In addition, distractions don't just eat up valuable time, they also diminish mental progress for up to thirty minutes. In other words, the sixty seconds one takes to check Facebook is a total of thirty-one minutes of work productivity gone.

The overall impact of distractors on mental well-being is even more compelling. Based on a comprehensive study, distractions lead to higher stress, increased blood pressure, bad moods, and lower productivity.

While the potential for distractions can occur anywhere, people leaders need to ask employees about the external distractions they may be dealing with remotely and offer ways to minimize them. For example, setting up specific times to review chat, email, and Slack notifications instead of reacting to a new ping every few minutes—ensuring employees are taking breaks, eating lunch away from all devices, setting up a clutter-free environment, creating a designated "office" zone, or playing white noise in the background. There needs to be extra care on the leaders' and employees' parts to discuss what is required and ensure that the remote environment is the most conducive to a sense of well-being and productivity.

Another subtle but notable Requirements weight buster when working remotely can be virtual or digital fatigue. According to Monster.com, 69% of employees are experiencing burnout symptoms while working from home. This represents a 20% increase in only three months. While burnout on its own refers to the state of mental, emotional, and physical exhaustion caused by chronic stress, virtual burnout or virtual fatigue is a specific type of burnout caused by the continuous and excessive use of digital devices.

People who work remotely tend to be tethered longer to their devices as their only way to ensure visibility and connectedness to others. This increased frequency can impact different feelings of burnout and add to the Requirements weight of always needing to be on.

It is not uncommon for many employees working remotely to experience a struggle with disconnecting from work, unlike employees who work on-site. Knowing when to switch off the workday becomes blurred when 24/7 access is an option. Gartner reports over 40% of employees in the hybrid world are 1.27 times more likely to struggle with disconnecting from work than those who work on-site. Forty percent of remote employees reported an increase in the length of their workday during the first nine months of 2021 when the study was conducted.

Many employees reported that their employers have installed tracking and monitoring systems to determine hours and online activities. Over 94% of employees who feel tracked are more likely to use decoys to make it appear they are working due to the pressure of always being on. Alexia Cambon, Gartner's Research Director, describes the perfect metaphor of what it's like to live with the cumulative issues of distractions, virtual fatigue, and always-on mentality:

> Imagine driving a car, and a squirrel jumps in front of your car every 40 seconds. That's your digital distraction. Now add a passenger next to you who won't stop talking. That's your virtual overload. Finally, put this car on a highway with no exit signs. That's your always-on mindset. So, you're in a car that's start-stopping every 40 seconds, with a passenger who won't stop talking, and there's no way to take it off the road. Wouldn't that make you tired?

LIGHTEN THE VIRTUAL MEETING LOAD

Online meeting fatigue is real, and leaders can unintentionally add to that Requirements weight with meeting times and lengths. People cannot sit in Zoom meetings hours at a time. Before holding the next one, see if you can lighten the meeting by asking these questions:

- **Is the meeting necessary?** Can the information be provided any other way? Does it need to be a weekly or biweekly meeting? If the meeting is not an effective use of time, cancel it. One of the most appreciated ways to help lighten the Requirements weight is to give back the gift of time.

- **Are the meetings the right length with adequate breaks in between?** For some companies, sprinting has become the new marathon and is impossible to sustain. Data show that the most productive virtual meetings should be no more than forty-five minutes, with a break of fifteen to twenty minutes in between to prepare and mentally regroup for the next one.

- **Is the purpose of the meeting, intended outcomes, and attendee list clarified?** Is there a plan? If not, attendees should have the right to ask for one and base their invite acceptance on the value they can add. Make sure you provide an agenda. It's an easy way to deliver more weight to the Respect side of the scale. Also, stick to the agenda times and have a timekeeper. There's nothing more disrespectful than asking someone on the spot to cut their hard-worked fifteen-minute presentation to five minutes because of running out of time. Or worse, telling them their presentation is tabled until next week's meeting.

KNOCK DOWN THE BUREAUCRATIC ROADBLOCKS

Another guaranteed way to add weight to the Requirements is with bureaucratic roadblocks. It feels hard to get work done in some organizations, like rolling a boulder uphill; it soon becomes exhausting even to care anymore. Top performers in particular have no patience for clunky workarounds, disjointed systems, or redundant processes with multiple entry/exit points and lack of adequate tools for team collaboration. They want streamlined technology that is dependable, stable, and easy to use. They also want processes that are simple and efficient, without excessive controls. When four approval levels are needed to credit a customer $20 or reimbursement for a $10 employee expense, the company's willingness to embrace an environment of trust and support is in jeopardy.

Employees want their company experience to be one of ease and empowerment, not bureaucratic boulders. When employees don't feel chained down by activities like processing endless reports or completing stacks of forms that don't add any value to the effectiveness of doing their job, they report being happier and more fulfilled. It's not uncommon to hear, "I loved my job when I got to do it; it was all the other stuff that got in the way of it that caused me to quit."

PERFORMANCE MANAGE FOR OUTCOMES AND RESULTS

Remote and hybrid models are a huge paradigm shift for leaders used to depending on optics as part of a way to determine an employee's performance such as observed time in the office rather than outcomes and results. When that mind shift isn't successfully made, the old command and control approach takes over and the result is online micromanaging to the point of using surveillance monitoring tools to track employees' every move and time-punched hour.

The immediate question is why. There isn't a more telling red flag of a culture of distrust, and such actions will not rescue you from the low performer. They will only alienate your best people.

In a study commissioned by ExpressVPN, in collaboration with Pollfish, 2,000 employers and 2,000 employees who work in a remote or hybrid capacity were surveyed to reveal the extent of employer surveillance and how it is impacting employees. Their findings noted that more than half of employees said they are likely to quit if their company and/or boss uses surveillance measures, and one-quarter would take a pay cut to avoid these tools. Being subjected to monitoring will add so much unnecessary weight to your top performers' Requirements side of their 3-R scale, they will eventually leave because of it.

WHAT EMPLOYEES ULTIMATELY WANT FROM REMOTE LEADERS

- Trust, trust, trust

- Extra, positive attention

- A say in the remote and hybrid policies

- Resources needed to achieve their goals

- Equal opportunity to express and be heard

- Clear digital rules: formal and informal

- Dependable technology

- Collaboration software

- Continual feedback: positive and constructive

- Opportunities to casually connect with coworkers

- Meetings with a purpose

- Easy, nonbureaucratic processes and policies

- Performance management-based results and outcomes

SUCCESSFUL REMOTE WORKING IS A TWO-WAY STREET

The success or failure of a remote working model goes both ways. The responsibility to ensure it is effective and productive for everyone falls equally on the remote employees' shoulders. Leaders who trust their people with autonomous ownership of their day and deliverables deserve the actions and behaviors in return that justify that trust. Just as successful remote leaders need a specific game plan for mindful connections, meaningful interactions, and ensuring opportunities for team connectivity, the remote employee needs to have the same game plan for their leader.

Help your people live up to their part in successfully maintaining a remote environment that works for all. Share these key guidelines with them:

- **Keep your leader proactively in the loop.** Provide project and process updates without waiting to be asked. Communicate often and purposefully.

- **Show initiative.** The most successful remote employees contribute strategic value in addition to just completing tasks. Most work is solving problems. Remote employees getting the most visibility are the ones who don't wait for directions but rather initiate ideas and creative ways to think through alternatives to solve issues. Make it a point always to add extra value in some way. Even if all suggestions are not adopted, the willingness to show initiative counts and helps to build your brand remotely.

- **Have a voice.** It can be frustrating for a leader on a virtual call to pose a question, ask for input, or solicit opinions and get nothing back but pixels of blank faces on mute. Don't be one of those faces. Speak up. Remote employees need to be more visible than their on-site counterparts, and that means offering an opinion and having a voice. Even if it's to validate and acknowledge a point already made—anything is better than silence.

- **Look the part.** As with on-site employees, the image still matters. People will always formulate a quick opinion of who you are based solely on their first impression of what they visually see of you, and that includes an online presence as well. If you're looking for promotability, take control of what you want that impression to be. That goes for your personal attire, grooming, and the appearance of your virtual background as well. An unmade bed or a messy closet or sink full of dishes is not the ideal backdrop. Check the blur background option if all else fails.

- **Create perceived proximity.** This is perhaps the biggest key to ensuring visibility when working remotely. Perceived proximity is the ability to create a cognitive sense that impacts the positivity of a relationship. In other words, make people feel like you're there, even though you're not. Point blank: remote workers must work at this. Proximity doesn't just happen by default. A couple of ways to begin is to communicate twice as often as you think you need to and in at least three different ways. With so many channel options, the best approach is to cover all of them. Have a presence everywhere— on collaboration tools, texts, email, project boards, blog posts, on the share site. Whatever the choices, mix up where you show up and do it often.

- **Be human.** Another way to create perceived proximity is to be human. Don't be all business, all the time. Remote workers don't have the advantage of reading body language and all the nonverbal ways people get to know each other. However, that doesn't mean that the need for remote workers to humanly know their leader and coworkers goes away. It just means that the remote employee desiring to be known will have to manage that outcome consciously and proactively. As appropriate, share photos or quick videos that tell others who you are as a person. Talking about hobbies, trips, kids, and pets are all examples to get a lens into the human side of the remote worker. If you cook, how about sharing a special recipe for the holidays? If you have a dog, maybe share a puppy training tip that worked for you. The topic is unimportant, but the point is to inject some three-dimensional humanness into a two-dimensional digital world.

REMOTE IN SOME CAPACITY IS HERE TO STAY

The remote working model is here to stay in some form for almost every knowledge worker. As a result, organizations need to take it upon themselves to start testing their inclusivity processes for remote workers. There's too much at stake to do anything less. A company's culture will be negatively impacted by the us-versus-them chasm creating a class system that will set up a sense of not belonging for the remote group and resulting in the inability to attract talent and keep them.

A strong culture with remote and on-site employees working collaboratively starts with leveling the on-site and remote availability options. In an interesting twist, some companies have begun to mandate that employees cannot be in the office five days a week and requires them to be remote for at least one day. This approach forces the organization to inspect further the quality and availability of their collaboration tools, communication processes, meeting protocols, mindful and consistent check-ins, recognition forums, and ways to keep the organization's mission and purpose at the forefront of all employees on-site and remote alike. It also helps to displace any stigma of being a remote worker when at some point all employees are one.

Keep in mind a few general ideas to navigate these tricky remote waters. Ensure remote tools and processes provide an equitable visibility field for on-site employees and remotes. Consider upgrading the collaboration software tools to create a full transparency exchange into everyone's work. Many planning and project management tools provide a real-time lens into what all team members are working on and invite collaboration and inclusive feedback from which all may benefit.

Take a position of all hands on deck where appropriate. There may be certain times when all employees must attend meetings in person.

If that's the case, a remote worker living within reasonable proximity should also be required to participate on-site. Where it makes sense, record virtual meetings for reviewing later. On-site employees attending remote meetings should log on from their workstations instead of collectively in a conference room where the meeting before the meeting and the meeting after the meeting are more likely to occur, creating the potential for feelings of exclusion for those not in the room.

Going forward, as remote working models become more the norm, leaders will want to take extra care and keep a watchful eye on ensuring those employees making the transition from on-site to remote, as well as those who are seasoned remote workers, are maintaining a decision scale that is balanced with all the Requirements, Rewards, and Respect they are experiencing as a result. From a leadership and organizational perspective, both groups must be equally supported.

TAKE FIVE

1. Recent studies looking at remote workers found that those who are most likely to succeed have a proclivity toward agreeableness. They take most events and outcomes in stride, focus on the positive, and are considered easy going. Those who are struggling are the ones who are highly alert to their surroundings and deal with an underlying turmoil of continual anxiety and pressure, which is only made worse working in an environment where the human factor is absent.

2. A trusting people leader and organizational culture is a nonnegotiable for any employee looking to join an organization today, particularly working remotely. Make trust your default outlook. Decide that you are going to come from trust first, until someone makes it clear they cannot be trusted.

3. Working remotely comes with an additional set of challenges that may add hidden weight to the Requirements side of an employee's balance scale. If leaders are not aware of them and on the lookout, they can quickly creep up on an employee's 3-R scale and create enough of an imbalance to cause them to quit when, all along, an astute leader could have managed the save.

4. Employee engagement is more at risk digitally than on-site, not only because of the potential for isolation but also due to the high level of outside distractions. Employees working in a remote world are 2.54 times more likely to experience digital distractions than on-site employees.

5. Have a well-planned strategy for a hybrid working option. Communicate it clearly and often so that everyone understands the expectations and guidelines.

SURVIVAL TACTIC #1
ADDITIONAL CHALLENGES OF REMOTE WORKERS

If you are leading remote team members, it is critical to take the time to fully understand the unique impact that working from home may have and how it's affecting the balance of their 3-R scale. For some it will be an ideal working environment and will not have a negative impact on their Requirements weight. Others may find that working remotely has additional and unexpected challenges.

Review the primary reasons for remote worker burnout to see if any of them resonate as you think about each of your remote workers. Ask them if they identify with any of the following challenges and mitigate as needed.

REVIEW ADDITIONAL CHALLENGES OF WORKING REMOTELY

REMOTE CHALLENGE	TEAM MEMBERS TO WATCH
Fear of missing out (FOMO)	
Feelings of loneliness	
Always needing to be on mentality	
Missing out on professional development opportunities	
Inadequate working environment	
Lack of discipline and accountability	

SURVIVAL TACTIC #2
REMOTE LEADER BEST PRACTICES

√	BEST PRACTICE
	I trust my employees until there's a reason not to.
	I provide extra positive attention.
	My team has a say in the remote and hybrid policies.
	My remote workers have the resources needed to achieve their goals.
	I allocate equal opportunity and time for my remote employees to be heard.
	I have communicated clearly defined digital policies such as cameras required when attending meetings, expectations for message response times, and online availability.
	My remote workers have been provided with dependable technology and equipment.
	Every remote worker has access to a robust and easy collaboration software.
	I provide continual feedback: positive and constructive.
	I regularly set up virtual opportunities to casually connect with coworkers.
	Required meetings have a purpose, and remote workers are clear what value they will contribute.
	The virtual processes to connect with the team and the organization are easy.
	I focus on their results not hours or monitoring software to determine their value and contributions to the business when assessing their performance.

SURVIVAL TACTIC #3
HYBRID STRATEGY PLAN

Defining your hybrid vision and setting up the guidelines to maintain it is an important part of a successful hybrid option. Make sure the rules and guidelines are clearly and consistently communicated so all members understand the expectations.

What are the guidelines that qualify a position to have a hybrid option?	
Is there a minimum number of on-site days required each week? If so, how many?	
Are the on-site days and remote days standardized for all hybrid workers or can they be customized per individual employee?	
If customized, can the on-site days and remote days change from week to week?	
Are there events such as team meetings that require hybrid employees to attend in person?	
Will on-site employees be required to attend all virtual meetings? At their own workstation, or together in a conference room?	
When hybrid employees are on-site, will they have a hot desk or independent workstation?	

When on-site, are hybrid employees held to the same office hours as on-site employees?	
If a hybrid worker isn't able to be on-site as expected, who does the employee inform and how are they notified?	
Do all hybrid employees have access to the same technology, equipment, and tools?	
What standards and metrics will be used to measure a hybrid employee's performance?	

17

EVERY EMPLOYEE IS A 3-R SCALE IN PROCESS

Leaders who adopt the desire to serve their teams and see their primary responsibility as what they can do for their people, instead of telling their people what they need to be doing for them, will be the ones to thrive in this new workplace.

Each of your employees is carrying around their own personal 3-R scale with your company name on it. Even the future new hires begin to set up their 3-R scale the minute they touch the company. Some of your employees' scales are nicely in balance. As soon as possible find out why and make sure they stay that way if you plan to keep them for the long term.

Other employees' scales are in a dangerous tilt right now because of Requirements that are too heavy and Rewards and Respect that are too light. Have a 3-R conversation immediately to clarify the Requirements that are putting weight on their energy physically, emotionally, psychologically, or socially, and in whatever other way that matters to them.

Do the same when asking them about their tangible Rewards. Are there even Rewards for them in the first place? What matters most when they consider any of the exchanges they may be getting in return for the work they are doing like paychecks, commissions, bonuses, profit sharing, healthcare packages, or student debt support, to name a few?

Last, have a 3-R conversation about the Respect they feel they are getting from you as their leader and the organization. Every time your top performer recalls a demonstration of your appreciation in a way most meaningful to them, it adds up on the Respect side. Every time you encourage your people to grow, risk, and be better than they were the today before, more Respect weight is added. Anytime you give your employee the message that you always have their back and care about them as a person, even more Respect weight is added.

Every small note, simple trinket, extra attention, clear communication, and successful coaching heaps even more on the Respect side of their 3-R scale. And for every one of those examples of Respect that you haven't shown, even the smallest load of Requirements just got a lot heavier.

People have always carried a 3-R scale into work; the pandemic just happened to be the Great Accelerator for balancing it. As people slowly come through the Great Wait and decide to come back to work at a new opportunity, employees will be more hyperalert than ever about what it's going to take to start out with a balanced scale and keep the scale in balance.

Organizations have tremendous power in setting up the potential for an employee's scale to balance beginning day one, and their people leader has even more ability to keep it in balance. When the business creates a strong and healthy culture that is demonstrated in its recruiting, interviewing, and onboarding process, employees see that as being authentic, and a solid foundation exists on which they want to place their scale.

The people leader owns the responsibility of sustaining the balance of the scale by holding frequent 3-R conversations with each employee to assess where any imbalances may begin to occur. Calibrating the balance of an employee's decision scale can be attained in two ways: lightening the perceived Requirements or increasing the weight of the Rewards and the Respect.

As the option of working remotely continues to take more ground and becomes a part of the everyday norm of doing business, leaders must care for it as a separate entity with its subculture and needs. Flexibility is king in this new world. Employees need a sense of control and choice to define how they can best show up to excitedly do their work and contribute to the organization in the most meaningful way with a balance of their overall well-being. The only rule anyone seems to be living by right now is that there is no rule to live by right now. Every norm, paradigm, policy, procedure, and way of doing anything is up for renewal and will likely need complete rewriting.

So while the dust continues to figure out where it wants to settle, let's revisit the most fundamental truth we can stand upon and be comforted, knowing that there are some truths that will never change. By now, the premise should come as no surprise, people are *people*, first, and they will always be first before anything else. Everything we do as people aims to meet these basic needs in one way or another. That includes workplace motivators and the behaviors we can observe as a result.

FINAL WORD: WHO OWNS EMPLOYEE RETENTION?

In several organizations when employee turnover becomes an issue, the first inclination is to direct HR to fix it, who happens to already be drowning with processing terminations and back-filling openings in addition to all the other tactical management pieces that need their daily attention. As a result, HR deflects the responsibility onto the people leaders for their lack of leadership skills that is driving people away. The people leaders in turn blame the organization for lack of training, resources, and no time to deal with their employees' burnout issues, not to mention trying to manage their own stress and stay sane through it all.

There's no one specifically at fault in this circular firing squad. Everyone has a case to make, but the ultimate loser in this blame game is the organization in terms of cost and lost productivity. So what's the answer to who should own employee retention?

On the surface it might appear the best response is that everyone in the company owns employee retention, and, yes, indirectly everyone in the company can influence it. But when everyone owns employee retention, ultimately no one owns it and that's where the challenge lies.

For most companies, employee retention is a shared partnership under the direction of the HR team who oversees recruiting, onboarding, and training. Departmental leaders may also have employee retention goals assigned to them. But if everyone owns only a little slice of responsibility for retaining talent and no one owns the coordination of all their independent efforts, it becomes less clear who ultimately has the responsibility for it.

I worked with an organization whose retention strategy was to double their fulltime recruiting staff of three recruiters to six, as a way to get ahead of their turnover issue. They were losing so many people during their first year of employment, the thought was to put the majority of their resources into hiring as many people as possible, as quickly as possible.

While the recruiting process is definitely a critical operation to attract and hire the right people to begin with, all I could picture by this endeavor was an already big revolving door spinning furiously with employees coming into the organization and just as quickly leaving the organization, and by doubling the recruiting staff, the door only got wider, and the revolving mechanism got a lot faster.

Treating the symptoms of employee churn is not a sustainable solution to get to the root of why people are wanting to leave in the first place.

Compare the approach of hiring additional recruiters with another company who recently created a new position titled Director of Employee Success. The focus of this role is to help anticipate and adapt what is needed for individual employees to feel empowered to do their best work and care for any concerns or issues that potentially could be in their way from doing so. The person in this role works closely with people leaders, recruiters, company brand marketers, and senior executives as well as HR to help define weak spots in the company's retention process and proactively anticipate and care for employees' welfare and any concerns.

Consider these activities as an example as part of this role's focus:

- Supporting people leaders in their 3-R leadership approach

- Assessing where additional people leadership training is needed

- Conducting stay interviews and aggregating themes for why people remain with the company

- Serving as an employee liaison to answer questions and collect feedback

- Working with compensation for equitable adjustments as needed

- Helping to identify brand marketing initiatives and culture development needs

- Ensuring the first-day experience and onboarding processes are nothing short of stellar for on-site and remote team members

Like that of a healthcare case manager who coordinates multiple medical providers, treatments, prescriptions, and interventions for someone in need of long-term medical care, a single entity for employee retention can watch and own the big picture by coordinating the smaller parts and be accountable for the best outcome. This is not to say, however, that every other person in the organization is still not accountable for employee retention. Keeping top talent should remain a focus for everyone in the same way customer service and company ambassadorship should be.

In this post-pandemic war for talent, the stakes are higher than ever before. The "I quits" continue at a startling rate, and almost every industry is facing an uphill battle to replace those top performers they have lost. The best resource of talent is the people already on the team, which makes employee retention more critical now than ever.

What is your employee retention strategy? What are you actively doing to keep your best people? Leaders who have watched multiple employees exit may be used to replying with, "Fine, just let them go," are finding that is not the strategy of choice right now. The pandemic has brought an onslaught of soul-searching questions workers are now asking like, "Is my boss toxic or supportive?" "Does this company stand for what I value?" "Is this culture real or fake?" "Am I paid fairly?" "Am I respected, appreciated, and valued?" "Am I fulfilled with a purpose?" "Am I growing?"

Over the next couple of years we are going to see this soul searching become a talent war like none other. It's going to take a whole new way of thinking and a completely different set of tools. Hopefully now you've got the concepts down and see the need to embrace the new rules of engagement to keep your best people. The bad news is you can't afford not to. The best news is you've got this, and you will do it.

Want to know how you did on answering the true/false questions at the beginning of the book?

I am confident that each of my top performers feels they are getting the right balance of respect and rewards in return for the work required of them.	**Answer: Depends!** If you answered true, that is awesome and keep it up. If you answered false, but have read the book, you now know what to do.
The team leader is primarily responsible for their employees' retention.	**Answer: False.** While the team leader is a huge influencer on their employees' retention, it's a partnership beginning with the highest level leader in the organization.
What employees want most right now is empathy.	**Answer: False.** It's a close second. What employees are currently asking for the most is to be treated like human beings.
Respect is defined differently by the person receiving it; therefore, I am aware of what it uniquely means to each of my employees.	**Answer: Depends!** If you answered true, that is awesome and keep it up. If you answered false, now you know how to hold a 3-R conversation to find out!
Remote employees need just as much attention as those on-site.	**Answer: False.** They need more of your attention to feel the same as if they were on-site.

FINAL SURVIVAL TACTIC
PERSONAL COMMITMENT

What were the top three points you took away from this book?

1. _____

2. _____

3. _____

List three commitments you will make in the immediate future to begin implementing a 3-R leadership approach.

1. _____

2. _____

3. _____

ACKNOWLEDGMENTS

Every journey an author takes is only made possible by the special people who are kind enough to accompany them along the way.

First and foremost, to my Lord and Savior, Jesus Christ, who said, "In all your ways acknowledge him and he will direct your path." (Proverbs 3:6) And He most certainly did!

My amazingly creative and talented husband, James Martin, for your love, insights, and never-ending respect.

Mom and Dad, who cheered me on and encouraged me every single day of their lives.

Dan Brady, my brother who shares my thirst for knowledge and robust debates.

Sandra Wendel, my priceless editor. My beta readers: Cindy Ashburn, Tom Ashburn, John Boyens, Everett Brandt, Ed Bray, Laura Close, Todd Dekruyter, Patty England, Daniel Galster, Ross Haycock, Amy Mather, Nancy Mathes, Chris Meyer, Laurie Morin, Danielle Neumeyer, Joshua Newman, Anh Dao Pham, and Catherine Rymsha. Your feedback was invaluable. Because of you, this book was truly transformed. Thank you!

Last, to my ninth-grade English teacher who always said I would write a book, and now I finally did. With gratitude, Miss Phelps, this one is for you.

ABOUT THE AUTHOR

Merrylue Martin is a celebrated people leadership strategist with over four decades of successfully working with global leaders from all types and sizes of organizations, to make their employees feel uniquely respected, appreciated, fulfilled, and engaged.

As a Fortune 100 senior executive, educational administrator, management consultant, and business owner, she has comprehensive experience in creating and delivering strategies that engage and retain top performers.

Merrylue is an honored graduate of the renowned Women's Leadership program at the Wharton School of the University of Pennsylvania. Her doctorate in organizational leadership and published dissertation from Pepperdine University uncovered the research that resulted in business and leadership practices that directly drive an employee's decision to stay or leave an organization.

She has leveraged that work along with her learning and development background to put valuable information into practical ideas and tools that all people leaders can immediately begin implementing to win the battle of attracting and keeping top-performing employees. She is President and CEO of the Job Joy Group, LLC, a people leadership consulting firm. Her primary message to all leaders and the organizations that support them is that people will always be *people*, first, and employees second.

When not working with people leaders, Merrylue enjoys interior design, dreaming up concoctions in her art studio, and writing puppet scripts for the preschool church crowd, who remain her toughest critics to date. She and her husband, James, enjoy being Gram and Gramps to twin girls and a new baby boy.